The Voice of Victims
The Voice of the Crucified

A Franciscan Perspective

David B. Couturier, OFM Cap.

Franciscan Institute Publications
2019

Cover Design by Jill M. Smith

ISBN 978-1-57659-435-3
E-ISBN 978-1-57659-436-0

Library of Congress Cataloging-in-Publication Data

Names: Couturier, David B., author.
Title: The voice of victims, the voice of the crucified : an invitation to Franciscan hope / David B. Couturier, OFM Cap.
Description: St. Bonaventure : Franciscan Institute Publications, 2019. | Includes bibliographical references and index.
Identifiers: LCCN 2019000381 | ISBN 9781576594353 (pbk. : alk. paper)
Subjects: LCSH: Church work with the poor--Catholic Church. | Francis, of Assisi, Saint, 1182-1226. | Franciscans.
Classification: LCC BX2347.8.P66 C68 2019 | DDC 282--dc23 LC record available at https://lccn.loc.gov/2019000381

Printed and bound in the United States of America.
Franciscan Institute Publications makes every effort to use environmentally responsible suppliers and materials in the publishing of its books. This book is printed on acid free, recycled paper that is FSC (Forest Stewardship Council) certified. It is printed with soy-based ink.

Dedication

This book is dedicated to my father,
Normand F. Couturier,
a victim of a midnight assault.
Left paralyzed for the rest of his life,
he read the Scriptures at night for consolation.
Rest in peace!

ACKNOWLEDGMENTS

The poet, Mewlana Jalaluddi Rumi, a 13th century Persian theologian and mystic, once wrote:

> Be with those who help your being.
> Don't sit with indifferent people, whose breath
> comes cold out of their mouths.
> Not these visible forms, your work is deeper.

I have been blessed with many who have helped me with my being and with my doing, those who are anything but indifferent to the suffering and hurts of the vulnerable in our world. I want to thank the Franciscan Sisters of Allegany and their congregational minister, Sr. Margaret Mary Kimmins, OSF. Their commitment to social justice has been inspiring.

I want to acknowledge the significant work that Joseph Chinnici, OFM, has done on the issues of sexual abuse and Franciscan leadership. He has stimulated new avenues of thought as I have tried to integrate his original historical insights with my own research in psychology and organizational development. He has my respect and gratitude.

I have been Dean and Professor of Theology and Franciscan Studies at St. Bonaventure University. I want to acknowledge the support of administrators, faculty, staff and students who pursue the University's Franciscan mission with passion. I thank especially the President of the University, Dr. Dennis DePerro, the Provost, Dr. Joseph Zimmer, and the Dean of Arts and Sciences, Dr. David Hilmey. I serve as Director of University Planning with two amazing colleagues, Dr. Michael Hoffman and Ms. Ann Lehman. Their dedication to excellence and the welfare of our students is inspiring.

I have also served for the past several years as the Dean R. Hoge Professor of Pastoral Planning and Church Management at the Graduate Theological Foundation in Mishawaka, Indiana. As an ecumenical research and study center, it serves the needs of practicing ministers with creativity and resilience. I have been privileged to be a reader for several dissertations and participated in discussions with many of the

Foundation's professors. These endeavors have been a blessing and stimulus to my own ongoing research.

My Capuchin brothers in the Province of New York and New England have always prodded me to be the best scholar, priest, friar and brother I could be. Our work as a Province has always been a humble service among the most poor and vulnerable in some of America's most challenging urban centers. I want to acknowledge two brothers in particular, Jack Rathschmidt OFM Cap. and John McHugh OFM Cap., who celebrate their 50th anniversary as priests in 2019. They have been inspiring mentors and I am grateful for their friendship.

I acknowledge the dedicated and prodigious work of my colleague in the Franciscan Institute at St. Bonaventure University, Ms. Jill Smith. Keeping pace with her commitment to excellence in the way we do business has been a joy.

My family remains my touchstone of grace. My sisters will understand this book's focus and the significance of the book's dedication. Listening to the cry of victims was a lesson our mother taught with singular courage. Being a victim of an unknown assailant was our father's personal tragedy, which he bore with patience and strength.

Table of Contents

Introduction

Amber's Story

Amber is a young woman from the Buffalo NY area in her twenties that I met through the work of the Franciscan Sisters of Allegany.[1] She was a pretty normal young woman who went to high school and had the same dreams as everyone else – college, a good career, and a loving family, until life took an unexpected and dangerous turn.

Like many in her generation, she tried drugs. The soft stuff first, a little weed here and there, and then the hard stuff, the kind that is tough to shake on your own. She got hooked and then she got scared. She hid what she was doing, especially from her family. They wouldn't understand and she couldn't bear the shame. And then, she got pregnant and became more desperate. She turned to the wrong friends who turned her over to the wrong guys, the kind of men who want to make lots of money without breaking a sweat, who walk around without a care in the world and without a conscience. Dangerous men!

After her child was born, Amber became something that would have been unimaginable to young women from her good neighborhood in Cheektowaga – she became a human slave in the sex trade. She became part of the vast network of men, women, and children around the world who are used as sexual slaves in an industry that is the second most profitable criminal activity after drug trafficking worldwide.[2] Reports put profits from human trafficking, sexual and forced labor, between $31.6 billion and $150 billion annually.[3]

---

[1] Some names and details of the stories in this book have been changed in order to protect the privacy of individuals involved.

[2] United Nations Office on Drugs and Crime. *Transnational organized crime: Let's put them out of business.* Available at https://www.unodc.org/toc/en/crimes/organized-crime.html.

[3] International Labour Organization. (2014). *Profits and poverty: The economics of forced labour*. Available at http://www.ilo.org/global/publications/ilo-bookstore/order-online/books/WCMS_243391/lang–en/index.htm; John Vanek, *The Essential Abolitionist: What you need to know about human trafficking and modern slavery* (Daliwal Press, 2016).

Over several conversations, Amber shared with me the terror of human trafficking – the loss of control over her everyday life, the constant degradation of her self-esteem and dignity, the limits placed by traffickers on her movements and decision-making, and the general feeling of hopelessness that overtakes and shrouds her world.

Amber told me that I could relate her story to whomever I wished, on two conditions. I needed to protect her anonymity and she wanted me to emphasize in every talk that she was never a prostitute. She didn't make the choice to sell herself. She was threatened by the men to whom she owed money -- they would kill her entire family, if she didn't do what they said. They were the kind of men who could easily injure or murder those who got in their way.

So, for months she was forced into the sex trade but not on the seedy side of town. She was "too pretty" for all that. She was forced to work on the upscale side of the city, serving businessmen visiting from out of town and husbands who didn't want to go home to the wife and kids just yet – the lawyers, managers, and retailers in town. She told me that she hated every minute of it. All of what she did was forced by fear. Her handlers knew where she lived. They knew where her daughter went for day care. They knew her Mom and Dad's home. Their beatings and their guns convinced her that they were dead serious.

Her drug issues also convinced her that she had no recourse to the police. She saw only two alternatives: on the street or in the prisons – until one night when she found a way to escape.

The night's routine was regimented. She would be transported under guard and constantly monitored from a van. Usually the doors of the van were locked on the driver's side to thwart any chance of escape. This one night, however, she realized that the driver had forgotten to lock the door. As they approached a red light in Buffalo, as the van slowed down, she quickly opened the van door and rolled out onto the busy street. Cars screeched out of the way. She was hurt but she just ran for her life, around corners, in the shadows and then out of sight. She got herself to an emergency room and started getting the help she needed. She found support services and protection and a path to recovery.

When I told her I would like to share her story, she asked me to tell those who read it, "that no woman would want this for herself." No woman would plan this for herself. She wanted others to know that she was not a prostitute. She wanted readers to understand what it is like to be enslaved in America today, controlled for the profit of men to whom she was nothing more than a commodity to be bought and sold on the open market for a few dollars an hour.

Amber has a fierce determination to become free and to be whole again. Amber does not want the spotlight; she still experiences a great deal of shame. She *does* want to be heard; she wants people to listen carefully to her story and the stories of young women and men like her who have been victimized and abused in a slave trade larger than any the world has previously seen. Her traffickers tried to break her will and to take away her voice, her ability to cry out in pain, to scream at her injuries, and to call out for justice. She wants her voice and those of others who have been abused to be heard.

As we talk, she wonders whether any one will find her story compelling, whether people will listen to the voice of this anonymous victim from the suburbs of Western New York. Amber is in college, learning to forgive herself for her mistakes but dedicated to helping other women and men being trafficked in the Buffalo area. She is peaceful with where she is and where she is headed. But, she wonders still – is anyone listening? Do people actually care? Are people interested in hearing the voice of victims and will that voice be strong enough to make a difference in a world of overwhelming violence and tremendous greed?

This book is an invitation to learn the dynamics of an active listening to the cry of the poor, as this is described in our Scriptures and tradition. It is an invitation to renew a church, mired in scandal and abuse, because it has been grossly negligent and, in some cases, criminally deficient in its failure and refusal to hear the poor and vulnerable. It is a call to Franciscan hope in imitation of Francis who becomes the crucified victim in his own period by listening to the cry of the poor in his time.

Over the years, as a priest, a Capuchin-Franciscan friar, and as a psychotherapist, I have heard many voices of victims – a "lost boy of Sudan" stolen for slave labor, women subjected to domestic violence, gay men bullied and degraded for their sexual orientation, African-Americans exposed to racial biases and structural inequalities time and time again, and individuals sexually assaulted, some even by priests. These are the victims behind this book, a large chorus of pain whose voices have often been ignored or muted in a society with a mad frenzy for profit and progress.

I choose in this work to go back into the Scriptures of our religion not to be evasive of the cries of victims, but to give resonance and affirmation to modern voices as the sound of God *screaming in the night.* Religion has too often taken on the voice of power and privilege. Its real roots, its original and genuine inspiration, however, are in the voice of the poor and powerless.

The question I want to ask in this small book is-- why don't we hear those cries more often and why don't we respond more appropriately when we see the pain and know the hurt of our sisters and brothers? Why are the voices of victims so easily drowned out by other priorities?

The Scriptures, as we will see, are clear. The cry of victims is the language of God. No one can come to God and no one can understand the God of the Hebrew and Christian scriptures without taking to heart the cry of the victims of history. The Judeo-Christian faith is the story of the vulnerable and abused liberated by a compassionate God who wishes to be in solidarity with them.

I want to address that story from a decidedly Franciscan perspective, because the Franciscan movement begins when a young soldier back from war and tortured by doubts, hears the voice of a crucified man in the church of San Damiano. That "voice" leads Francis to go in search of the lepers that disgusted him throughout his youth and, for the first time in his life, to hear and recognize them as sisters and brothers. The fraternal dialogue that day becomes the premier healing movement of the Middle Ages.

This book revolves around a central thesis. The renewal of the Catholic Church depends on a conversion toward the victims of history. Cardinal Sean O'Malley OFM Cap. has put the stakes for the Church and its leadership starkly on the line, when he said: "Catholics have lost patience with us and civil society has lost confidence in us."[4]

The Church can no longer hide from the question that screams from all its recent court filings, legal documents and theological laments – why did we not hear the cries of the victims? Why did we not take notice of the "vox victimarum?" What theological priorities and pastoral preoccupations took precedence and seemed more important than those of victims? How do those preoccupations look in the light of the Scriptures we reverence and the rituals we perform?

Many bishops and religious leaders still seem to get it wrong. Their long and repetitive litanies of lament suggest that they believe the world wants to know that they are ashamed and repentant. It seems to me that mature adults want an answer to one central question – *why did you not hear the cry of the victims?*

You are shepherds. You are priests and bishops. You know the Scriptures. The question is: *What kept you from hearing the screams, the groans, the wailing and weeping of those abused in our churches and rectories?* And more -- *Why did it take lawyers to make you see and journalists to make you listen to what the Gospels pronounce as Christianity's first obligation to*

[4] Cardinal Sean O'Malley, August 17, 2018, https://zenit.org/articles/cardinal-sean-omalley-there-are-times-when-words-fail-us/.

notice, pay attention and take action on behalf of the widows and orphans, Lazarus at the gate and the Jew thrown into the ditch?

We are facing an awful truth: we silenced victims, when they cried out for help. The church of victims, of the beloved victims of God, closed its eyes, ears and heart to the many voices of victims who came for help and sought justice.

And now, the silencing of the victims must become deafening to us. If Amber's voice is one of the few voices we hear, it should be recognized that there are millions more in the world, thousands more in our churches just like her, bearing the scars and trying to heal the wounds of what has been done to them.

Let us not be naïve. The victims of abuse in the church are the first wave of witnesses, survivors of the horrors that continue elsewhere in our schools, businesses, military establishments, government agencies and family homes around the world.

The cry of the victims must become deafening to us. We must hear it with every fiber of our being, until we understand its significance before the law and before the living God.

The silencing of victims is now the shame of our religious history. We must now learn how to make the voice of the victims our predominant priority.

We will hear their cry in all its trauma and terror, when we are ready to admit that tending to that cry is the first task of Christianity in the 21st century. Our task in this book is to shake our lethargy and theologically scandalous complicity in ignoring, missing or muffling the sounds of suffering. We must open our Scriptures again and hear the voice of the crucified not as an easy tool for forgiveness or as a "cheap grace" for redemption, but as it truly is, the voice of God in our time reclaiming the world for goodness and justice once and for all. Until then, we must recast our theological systems and reset our church priorities to the "vox victimarum" so that it becomes our pathway to the divine and the renewal of the beloved community of God. This book is a small contribution to that adjustment so long overdue.

Questions for Reflection

1. Human trafficking is the second most profitable illegal trade after drugs. Why do you think it receives so little political and religious attention?

2. What of Amber's voice comes through our brief presentation? What inspires or challenges you?

3. What theological priorities have taken precedence over the cry of victims? Why is that so?

4. What discussions has your local church or community had regarding sexual abuse and human trafficking?

Chapter One

A Culture of Cruelty and Corruption

The Church is in crisis.[1] Almost twenty years after the sexual abuse scandal first broke in Boston, we find ourselves mired again in the ugly and terrifying realization that thousands more children have been abused than we were aware, more victims have been abandoned, families torn apart, and crimes committed and covered up by "men of God."[2] We now know that these crimes reach across the world to the highest levels of the Church, and include bishops, archbishops and cardinals. There is no doubt now that the Church has created a culture of corruption and cruelty against the people of God. We know that our litanies of shame

[1] This text is adapted from an article that appeared in *Franciscan Connections* 68: 3 (Fall 2018), 2-5

[2] It is important that we understand clearly the data around the incidence of child sexual abuse before and after its revelations in Boston in 2002. Mark Gray, a researcher for the Center for Applied Research in the Apostolate (CARA), recently provided important statistics about old and new cases. He writes: "The most common decade of birth for alleged abusers was the 1930s and the most common decade of ordination was the 1960s. This profile has not changed in allegations that emerged in the 14 years that have followed- including the recent grand jury report. No new wave of abuse has emerged in the United States." Gray goes on to compare the US Church's efforts to create safe environments with those of secular institutions. "In the last three years, 22 allegations of abuse occurring during 2015-2017 have been made. This is an average of about seven per year nationwide in the Church. That is far too many. Nothing is acceptable other than zero. At the same time, to put those reports in some context, 42 teachers in the state of Pennsylvania, where the grand jury reported from, lost their licenses to educate for sexual misconduct in 2017. As recently as 2015, 65 teachers in the Los Angeles Unified School District (LAUSD) were in "teacher jail" for accusations of sexual abuse or harassment in that county alone. The current wave of "educator sexual misconduct" has yet to receive the same aggregation and attention that clergy sexual abuse has by the media (although The Washington Post has rung a warning bell and Carol Shakeshaft has written extensively on it in academic work). As the John Jay researchers note, "No other institution has undertaken a public study of sexual abuse and, as a result, there are no comparable data to those collected and reported by the Catholic Church" (p. 5). See: Mark Gray, "Pain Never Disappears from Unhealed Wounds," (Georgetown University: CARA) August 28, 2018. Accessed at: http://nineteensixty-four.blogspot.com/2018/08/pain-never-disappears-from-unhealed.html.

and sorrow ring hollow and our procedures have been ineffective because they have protected bishops from accountability and transparency. It is clear that it was naïve at best and self-serving at worst for the bishops to have exempted themselves from the strict accountability protocols they imposed on priests during the development of the Dallas Charter in 2002. They relied on the principle that they answered to a higher power and jurisdiction in the Vatican, when they knew full well that the Vatican was ill-equipped to handle episcopal malfeasance of such a scope and magnitude. We are left with our horror, anger and rage. Archbishop Wilton Gregory of Atlanta recently spoke frankly and in personal terms that many of us can relate to:

> My anger and disappointment, shared by Catholics and others, are only heightened by the reality that leaders who have engaged in or neglected to protect others from such damaging and deviant behavior have for many years failed to be held accountable — and have even risen in leadership positions. We must do better — for the sake of all victims and survivors of sexual abuse, and for the sake of everyone whom we serve in the name of Jesus Christ.[3]

How did the Church in America, meant to be the "community of the beloved," turn into a culture of corruption and cruelty? How did it become possible for priests to attack their own parishioners, especially the youngest and most innocent among them, and for bishops to leave these victims in the ditch of their deepest pain against every moral norm and example of Jesus in the Scriptures? How could these bishops read the parable of the Good Samaritan and not feel indicted and compelled to compassion? How were they blind to their own cruelty? Part of the answer may lie in the failure of our bishops to understand how they have created and sustained a culture of indifference and privilege among themselves.

Several months ago, I read the entire transcript of the Australian Royal Commission's Final Report on the Institutional Responses to Child Sexual Abuse (December 15, 2017).[4] I was particularly intrigued by the grilling that the Archbishops of Australia took from the lead investigators. One question from a brilliant woman barrister stood out. Paraphrasing

---

[3] "Archbishop Wilton D. Gregory's Statement in response to the resignation of Theodore McCarrick," August 9, 2018, at: https://georgiabulletin.org/news/2018/08/archbishop-wilton-d-gregorys-statement-in-response-to-the-resignation-of-theodore-mccarrick/.

[4] Accessed at: https://www.childabuseroyalcommission.gov.au/document-library.

her question, it went something like this – you, Archbishops, have testified that you did not design a common national policy or procedure to deal with sexual abuse cases. Each diocese and each bishop developed individual and separate procedures. How is it, then, that all of you developed similar procedures and practices that look strikingly alike, despite never having spoken about this in common?

The Archbishops offered sincere responses, but they failed to answer the question. They couldn't answer it, because it would require a level of corporate understanding that most of us, in our highly individualized mindset, have failed to achieve. Dioceses, like all other institutions (secular and religious) are run by conscious and unconscious processes. There are institutional codes of conduct and rules of expectation that are conscious and find their way into our human resource manuals and there are other organizational codes, customs, attitudes and expectations that are unconscious and out of direct awareness.[5] Many of the codes on how to deal with power, anger and intimacy lie well below the normal levels of corporate discussion. These are the codes now coming to light as a result of sexual abuse cases and the #MeToo Movement.[6]

Bishops, like many corporate leaders, are woefully unaware of or indifferent to their own powerful aspirations and their attendant anxieties over weakness and loss of control. They are unaware as to how these anxieties and defenses become socialized in their institutions and routinized in leadership styles and structures.

Case in point. Theodore McCarrick was a troubled man for most of his priesthood and all of his time as bishop, archbishop and cardinal. And no brother bishop saw it? No fellow archbishop or cardinal had a clue? Or, is the problem deeper? One could argue, as socio-analysts trained in organizational defenses would, that they didn't want to see what they saw and know what they knew, because the anxiety over their failing system of leadership was too intense and threatening.[7] As Franciscan brothers and sisters, we must ask another question of ourselves – how did we not hear the cry of the victims and how did we not see that our bishops were becoming blind?

---

[5] David B. Couturier, "The Socio-Analytic Study of Catholic Organizations Today," in John H. Morgan, *Foundation Theology 2016* (Mishawaka, IN: The Graduate Theological Foundation, 2016), 43-54.

[6] David B. Couturier, "#MeToo and Franciscan Values: The Psychological, Organizational and Spiritual Dynamics of Sexual Harassment at Work," *Franciscan Connections* 68:1 (Spring, 2018), 31-40.

[7] Ken Eisold, *What you don't know you know: Our Hidden Motives in Life, Business and Everything Else* (New York: Other Press, 2009); Manfred F.R. Kets de Vries, *Struggling with the Demon: Perspectives on Individual and Organizational Irrationality* (Madison, CT: Psychosocial Press, 2001).

Truth and Reconciliation

There is a deeper lesson to be learned, one that can break through the anger, frustration, and sadness we feel. As Darleen Pryds indicated in a recent edition of *Franciscan Connections/The Cord,* Franciscans can be angry and sometimes must get angry in order to face the hardest and cruelest of truths.[8] And yet, anger can easily harden into a dead-end. As Franciscans we are by nature reconcilers and peace-makers. We thus must walk the difficult path by which we come to peace. Our South African sisters and brothers found a way to own, understand and begin to reform their apartheid past through their "truth and reconciliation" process.[9] Though not perfect, their honest confrontations with past injustices and their attempts at restorative justice have been replicated worldwide, exposing the hardest of truths while at the same time rebuilding relationships. Franciscans can help in the architecture by which the narratives of victims are fully heard and our systems and structures are turned toward reconciliation instead of an intractable sense of defensive protection and secrecy.[10]

New models of crisis resolution in church crises are emerging. The Leadership Conference of Women Religious has recently published a valuable series of reflections on a contemplative way of making meaning (as groups) in a time of crisis.[11] We must have the courage to tell the truth and be about the work of peacemaking. In reconciliation, someone has to go first and begin to speak. Clearly, victims have started to give voice to their pain. Perhaps we as Franciscans can learn how to listen fully, carefully, and compassionately. Perhaps we must also begin to speak our uncomfortable truths, even to bishops, but in a deeply Franciscan way.

This is not easy for us. Our Franciscan tradition reminds us to have a high regard for priests and bishops. At the same time, however,

---

[8] Darleen Pryds, "Can Franciscans Be Angry," *Franciscan Connections/The Cord* 68:2 (Summer, 2018).

[9] L. Allais, "Restorative Justice, Retributive Justice, and the South African Truth and Reconciliation Commission," *Philosophy & Public Affairs*, 39: 331–363 (2011). doi: 10.1111/j.1088-4963.2012.01211.x; A. Allan & M.M. Allan. "The South African Truth and Reconciliation Commission as a Therapeutic Tool," *Behavioral Sciences and the Law*, 18 (2000), 459-477.

[10] Bennett Collins, "Examining the Potential for an American Truth and Reconciliation Commission," (Carnegie Council on Ethics in International Affairs, February 5, 2015) examines several American adaptations of the South African TRC model, accessed at: https://www.carnegiecouncil.org/publications/ethics_online/0102.

[11] Annmarie Sanders, IHM, ed., *However Long the Night: Making Meaning in a Time of Crisis* [A Spiritual Journey of the Leadership Conference of Women Religious] (LCWR, 2018).

our brotherhood and sisterhood require us now to be forthright with them about their use of power, without arrogance but as a signal of our compassion and understanding. There are truths we know and a reconciliation we believe is possible.

WHAT DO WE KNOW?

Our Franciscan movement began in a time of deep crisis. Francis and Clare knew intimately the corruption of power in their own families and in society. As an alternative, Francis and Clare developed the modality of minority, with an emphasis on humility, transformative mutuality and compassionate dialogue, to break through the stalemate of greed and violence that had infected the clerical and social power of their day. Because of our heritage, Franciscan minority has always led us to an uncomfortable truth: there is a toxic aspect to our clerical system of government that leads us to misuse power and misunderstand intimacy. Joseph Chinnici OFM has detailed the particular organizational ascetics that Franciscans use to mitigate this danger.[12] Those ascetics lead us to a different perspective.

Once again, McCarrick is an example, not a scapegoat. He is a charming and immensely talented man who, I am sure, deeply loves God and wants to serve that God. And yet, he is, if reports are true, a deeply troubled man. And, I believe, he is a profoundly lonely and isolated man whose power and ambition blinded his fellow bishops from seeing what was going on for so long and right in front of them.

McCarrick's fellow bishops couldn't see how he used his power to force intimacy and his ambition to avoid his anxieties. Bishops have an opportunity (and we should lovingly help them) to learn something about the toxic nature of their own power and ambition and how it keeps them from seeing what is right in front of them and from acting effectively and ethically for those they are ordained to serve.

There is a hard and troubling truth staring us in the face. Those of us who lead the church and its ministries at its various levels (bishops, priests, religious women and men) do not understand or are profoundly ambiguous about the relational dynamics of power and intimacy both personally and organizationally. We have known this since the groundbreaking studies on the psychological forces in vocational life

---

[12] Joseph P. Chinnici, *When Values Collide: The Catholic Church, Sexual Abuse and the Challenges of Leadership* (Maryknoll, NY: Orbis Books, 2010).

were first published in the 1970s and 1980s.[13] Our ambivalence over these results and what they tell us about desire in religion continues to hamper our ability to proceed effectively toward the personal and structural conversion we need. But there is hope and a deeply Franciscan hope, within the structures of our minority and prophetic presence.

The Franciscan Movement began with a divine mandate to "repair the churches." St. Francis stood before the cross at San Damiano and heard the charge to attend to the ruinous dynamics affecting the church of God in his day. His efforts and the legacy he left were not a recitation of "shame and sorrow." It was a life of penance, which went beyond the occasional act of fasting or intense prayer.[14] Francis changed structures. He transformed his life, his behaviors and the very architecture of his life from privilege to poverty, from hubris to humility. He developed a new form of life, one of social engagement organized around minority and a fraternal economy[15]. None of us will succeed by intoning litanies of shame and sorrow. People need and deserve to see actions that reflect a new minority among those who have been accustomed to privilege and prestige. That transformation will not be easy, but it is possible.

The Church loves the Lord and depends on His grace. There is no doubt about this and this truth still comforts, consoles, moves and inspires the people of God. However, the church also wrestles with the ambiguities that tempt us to hide failures behind patterns of secrecy and protection. If we are to surpass this moment of unparalleled crisis, we will have to confront our inordinate and inconsistent affliction with power and intimacy. We will need to forego the temptation to scapegoat others for what is our distinct crisis and blindness. Organizational psychologists already see the danger of our familiar patterns of avoidance – i.e., splitting the world into ideologies of "all good" and "all bad." This crisis deserves better than tired tropes that blame this horror on "them," whether liberals or conservatives, or any targeted group put in danger of illogical and unsubstantiated discrimination once again (i.e., homosexuals).[16] What is

[13] L.M. Rulla, J. Ridick and F. Imoda, *Entering and Leaving Vocation: Intrapsychic Dynamics* (Rome: Gregorian University Press,1987) and *Psychological Structure and Vocation: Motivations for Entering and Leaving Vocation* (Dublin: Villa Books, 1979).

[14] R. Stewart, *De Illis qui faciunt Penitentiam. The Rule of the Secular Franciscan Order: Origins, Development, Interpretation.* (Rome, Istituto Storico dei Capuccini, 1991).

[15] David B. Couturier, "Franciscan Minority and Prophetic Presence: A Psychological Perspective," in E. Covi, *Francescanesimo e Profezia* (Rome, 1985), 664-673 and *The Fraternal Economy: A Pastoral Psychology of Franciscan Economics* (South Bend, IN: Cloverdale Books, 2007).

[16] Kathleen McChesney, "What Caused the Crisis?: Key Findings of the John Jay College Study on clergy sexual abuse," *America* (June 6, 2011) accessed at: https://www.americamagazine.org/faith/2011/06/06/what-caused-crisis-key-findings-john-jay-col-

at issue are the unconscious ways that power and intimacy at the highest levels of the Church interfere regularly with our deepest aspirations. The quicker we confess this and learn how this comes to be, the faster will be our repair.

St. Francis provided an answer to the crises of his time. He provides an answer for the ecclesial crisis of our age. It lies in a new spirit of minority, which begins with a humble, empathic and dialogic truth-telling. St. Francis was not afraid of this scandal of confession and the reform it requires. Nor should we be. I share the hope and prayer of Archbishop Wilton Gregory:

> I pray that this moment, and these days, weeks, and months ahead, will be an opportunity for light to break through the darkness, and for darkness to be exposed to the light. I pray that all victims and survivors of sexual abuse will come forward and receive the help, support, and healing they need. And I pray that our Church and our leadership will be renewed and transformed by the light of Christ and have the courage to take the necessary next steps.
>
> Like so many of you I am angry, but I am not overcome by despair. I hope and I pray that the Holy Spirit will cleanse and strengthen the Church. My anger has not led me to hopelessness; I pray yours has not either. I am grateful for your witness of faith and hope, even in difficult times.[17]

---

lege-study-clergy-sexual-abuse; see the (unsubstantiated) words of Bishop Robert Morlino, in Brian Rowe, "Bishop Morlino, others charge 'homosexual subculture' for clergy sexual abuse crisis." in *National Catholic Reporter* (August 21, 2018), accessed at: https://www.ncronline.org/news/accountability/bishop-morlino-others-charge-homosexual-subculture-clergy-abuse-crisis and Dr. Thomas Plante, "Continuing to blame homosexual men, celibacy, and believing that the frequency of clergy abuse found in the past (especially committed in the 1960's through the early 1980's) will continue now and in the future is clearly misguided based on these conclusive research findings," see "The New John Jay Report on Clergy Sex Abuse," *Psychology Today* (May 18, 2011), accessed at: https://www.psychologytoday.com/us/blog/do-the-right-thing/201105/the-new-john-jay-report-clergy-abuse-in-the-catholic-church.

[17] Wilton D. Gregory, op. cit.

Questions for Reflection

1. What reaction did you have to the statement that "the church has created a culture of corruption and cruelty against the people of God?"

2. Darleen Pryds suggests that there are times when Christians and Franciscans must get angry. What angers you in the Church today? What disappoints and frustrates you? What are healthy ways to channel that anger?

3. How did Francis of Assisi "repair the church" in his day? How would that repair look like today?

Chapter Two

Victims in the Brickyards of Egypt

Cardinal Luis Antonio Tagle of Manila tells the following story about Pope Francis when he came to Manila in January, 2018, and spoke with young people:

> A boy and a girl, both street kids now living in a shelter, recounted their harrowing stories. The young girl, Glyzelle, addressed the pope in Filipino and burst into tears at the end of her speech. Pope Francis asked me what the girl had said and why she was crying. I translated her words for the pope: "Why does God allow the suffering of children?" Pope Francis departed from his prepared text and said, "Only when our hearts can ask this question and weep can we begin to understand. Let us learn to weep the way Glyzelle taught us today."[1]

In the Winter 2018 issue of *Franciscan Connections/The Cord*, Joseph Chinnici of the Saint Barbara Province of OFMs offered an extended meditation on the question of the revitalization of Franciscan life today.[2] His backdrop was the merger of the Friars Minor of Canada into a single province and the decision of the majority of OFM provinces in the United States to merge into one province, as well. Chinnici is cautious about these merger efforts, not because he does not think structures need to be changed and religious organizations do not need to be more efficient. It is because (and I hope I am paraphrasing him well), he fears that these organizational restructuring efforts will not sink deeply enough into our Franciscan soul and will not truly "revitalize" Franciscan life today.

These mergers are, he fears, dangerous temptations to an unfortunate possibility: despondency and despair when nothing seriously changes, after all our work. We could experience a kind of institutional sugar-high

---

[1] Joshua J. McElwee, Cindy Wooden, eds., *A Pope Francis Lexicon* (Collegeville, MN: Liturgical Press, 2018), 184.

[2] Joseph P. Chinnici, "Passing on the Seal of Franciscan Life: What Revitalization Means," *Franciscan Connections/The Cord* 68:4 (Winter, 2018), 4-21.

when energy spikes and then crashes, as we "right size" the Provinces only to find that nothing much has changed at all.

Chinnici is arguing for a more incisive integration of the spirit, one that takes us deeply into the mystery of our own suffering, isolation and frustration over these many years. He is readying and steadying us now that religious life faces its most severe challenges in centuries. Chinnici wants us to face these difficulties head on, to shoulder these burdens directly. He holds the conviction that hope is found at the core of darkness and difficulty. Here is how Chinnici writes about the journey to hope through difficulty:

> What our stories indicate, what oil represents, is the vitality that comes from a revitalized sense of who we are as human beings and as friars minor. It is a "fountain within us", an inexhaustible source, "a hope that will not leave us disappointed, because the love of God has been poured out in our hearts through the Holy Spirit who has been given to us." (Rom. 5.5; see Jn. 4.14). Embarking on our journey, we experience in ourselves the passing of things: people, places, commitments, inheritances, a whole lifetime of work scuttled on the shoals of history; but we will discover in a surprising way that the good things we treasure are still there, in our memory, protected forever by the re-membering that is God's love for us. Good things fought for over time do not die, they simply go underground, germinate, mutate into new forms, and wait for a more propitious change in climate to reemerge in transformed but recognizable shapes. Why? Because God's care has not diminished, his faithfulness has not failed. He who has led us along the way, blessed our undertakings, indeed provoked us into embarking on this journey as friars minor and as human beings; he who has written our identity in the palm of his hand, has only been purging us of our illusions, our pretenses about our own importance, our necessities of being right, our plans for making an impact—and he has done this only so that in His grace we might affirm ourselves as free, grateful, reconciled, and on mission. Paul notes in his greeting to the church in Philippi: "I am confident that the one

> who began a good work in you will continue to complete it until the day of Christ Jesus." (Phil. 1.6) As we shall see, the strength and the power of the risen Christ grasped now in a new way through a life of faith, hope, and love will continue to be our calling and mission in the world. Our journey is a process of reclaiming, purification, and new witness.[3]

What Chinnici is arguing for is a deep engagement with our disappointments and disillusionments, our difficulties and our scandals because it is precisely in those places that we will find grace. He says it gracefully:

> What we need to remember, I believe, is that while our present world may be marked by poverties, the very things we identify as poverties point to solidarities that are much more profound. They indicate an emerging awareness that things should be different; they position us to be with the spiritually poor; and they point to great possibilities and to the heartfelt desire for the emergence of a new religious culture. We need to reverse the negative and see the signs of life embedded in this very discomfort with institutions, dogmatic pronouncements, and sacramental migration.[4]

This is Chinnici's most intriguing insight. In order to revitalize, our first task is not to plan or to form new committees to set goals, test assumptions, survey ideas and write objectives. Chinnici argues that these might become nothing more than abstract distractions. (Now that is a bit painful for someone who has spent his life helping religious to plan.) However, let's hear him out. His knowledge of Franciscan history and his experience of leadership in difficult times gives us reason to trust his insights.

What we need to do as a first step of revitalization, he suggests, is to *recover the memory* of who we are as human beings, what we are called to be, and what we are supposed to be about. This means finding ourselves, our identity and purpose in God again.

You may be saying to yourself – all that seems obvious and frankly redundant. What have we been doing all these years? Have we not been

[3] Joseph P. Chinnici, "Passing on the Seal of Franciscan Life," *Franciscan Connections* 68:4 (Winter, 2018), 4-21.

[4] Ibid, 8.

recalling, re-envisioning, re-imagining, and remembering so much of our past? Some might suggest – enough of nostalgia! It is time for new action, radically new action, that gets us moving beyond our circular debates about the past. It is time to claim a future and an adventurous one, at that!

It is interesting to note and important to learn that so much of our progress and our leaning into the future has been premised on our ability to forget and unlearn the past.

We have been trained philosophically and theologically to forgetfulness, to leave the past solidly and surely in the past.[5] Even as religious, although we carry many rituals and doctrines forward, we have been educated to a culture of amnesia. As a church historian, Chinnici is ready to admit that "the post-conciliar world in many instances was premised on the disavowal of the pre-conciliar inheritance."[6]

We thought that only by forgetting what we had inherited from the Middle Ages could we hope to move securely into a brighter future. Forgetfulness was the assurance of a transfigured history and a renewed future. Our unassailable confidence in progress helped us to jettison our roots and disown too much of our Catholic past. Our loss of religious memory, Chinnici reminds us, "made us vulnerable to modernity's forgetfulness."[7] Modernity's take on memory has a strange and unique pedigree.

In a sense, we got tricked and snookered into believing that a bit of forgetfulness of the origins of our Catholic and Franciscan history would open us to the brighter promises and deeper hopes ready to be taken up by a progressive and optimistic narrative. However, modernity's hold on time is stranger and more troubling than we understood and can tolerate.

Modernity is premised on the requirement that we forget a lot, perhaps too much:

> to forget the violence imposed on people by religious colonization; to forget the abusive activities of the clergy; to forget the harm done to the indigenous; to forget ourselves in a sea of external stimuli; to forget the misuse of power in inherited systems and institutions; to forget our own past complicity in sinful

[5] Francis O'Gorman, *Forgetfulness: Making the Modern Culture of Amnesia* (New York: Bloomsbury Academic, 2017).

[6] Chinnici., 9.

[7] Ibid.

> structures. To be modern is to forget the past and to embark on the quest for a new order of things.[8]

Having constructed a culture of amnesia, we stand as a civilization with our memories scrubbed of deficit and deficiencies in the blind hope of "inevitable human progress." We are left with what post-modernism provides – power dynamics and polarization, our isolation in search of profit.[9]

Our task now is to remember, to retrieve our deepest and first memories as children of God. It is in those memories that we will find our greatest hope, our deepest promise and our most secure path to the future. Our first memory as Christians, therefore, takes us to the brickyards of Egypt, where Scripture actually begins and Jews first encounter the God of Israel in action.[10]

IN THE BRICKYARDS OF EGYPT

How do we as Christians and as Franciscans remember? Where do we begin? How do we start? I believe that we must go back, not to Eden, but to the place where our religious history actually begins, in Egypt and in the hot sands and dangerous trails of Northern Africa.[11] Let me first take you to a recent event and then we will move further back in time.

Mohamed Bouazizi was a 26-year-old fruit seller in Tunisia. He did not have a city permit to sell his fruit and vegetables. He did not have the government's permission to earn a living to feed his impoverished family of seven. The police, known for their widespread corruption, confiscated his fruit cart and scale and physically assaulted him. He went to the governor's office to complain about the constant harassment and assaults he endured at the hands of deeply corrupt petty officials. He appealed to authorities but the officials there refused to see him or hear his complaint. He went outside, poured paint thinner on his body and lit the match.

---

[8] Chinnici provides us with some citations for further reference. David Gross, *Lost Time: On Remembering and Forgetting in Late Modern Culture* (Amherst, MA: University of Massachusetts Press, 2000)," as cited in Robert Orsi, "'The Infant of Prague's Nightie': The Devotional Origins of Contemporary Catholic Memory," U.S. *Catholic Historian* 21.2 (Spring 2003), 1-18, citation on 16.

[9] Zygmunt Bauman, *Postmodernity and its Discontents* (Malden, MA: Polity Press, 1997).

[10] Walter Brueggemann, "Action in the Brickyard," in Walter Brueggemann, *Peace* (St. Louis, MO: Chalice Press, 2001), 55-64.

[11]Walter Brueggemann, "The Alternative Community of Moses," http://teacherrenewal.wiki.westga.edu /file/view/Prophetic+Imagination.pdf.

With that gesture, Mohammed Bouazizi started the Arab Spring, the pro-democracy movement that sprang up throughout Northern Africa in the spring of 2011, which demanded democratic forms of government in the Middle East and the end of dictatorial regimes.

Deep in his soul, Mohammed knew what every oppressed man and abused woman must come to know: *There comes a time when enough is enough, when all the Pharaohs must fall.* The moment of conversion happens when we learn the lesson that all the Pharaohs who have hardened their selfish and greedy hearts against us must fall or we will never be free.

The moment of redemption comes in us when we learn that, no matter how strong they may be or how long they have reigned among us, it is God's will that the Pharaohs who have used and abused us are beholden to a new command from Yahweh to let us go free.

Our first memory as Christians, as it is for Jews, is that of slaves and victims in the brickyards of Egypt. It is there that we suffer; it is there that we cry to our strange God, that solitary God among the gods of Egypt, distant to us and silent among us for the last 400 years of our oppression at the hands of Pharaoh and his entire Egyptian conspiracy.

What we remember is the unbelievable moment when God hears the cry of the poor and the oppressed in Egypt. Unfortunately, we have so domesticated this moment in our religious imagination that we hardly feel its incredible urgency and its amazing disruption of ordinary order. Our religious health requires that we be shocked again by what we are being told about the gods of Egypt and the God of Israel.

It is not in the nature of ancient gods to hear or to notice the cry of the poor. The tales told of the gods remind us that they are involved in their own messy and chaotic lives, in their own parade of wars and storms, their charades of treacheries and adulteries, tempests and demotions.[12] They had more than enough to worry about than to become involved in the trivial aches and pains of the lowest and the least of humankind. Largely, the gods of the ancient world despised and dismissed humanity, which did not stop them from taking advantage of the poor. Mary Lefkovitz in a NY Times article, entitled "Greek Gods, Human Lives," summarizes the attitudes of all the ancient gods well, when she says, "Zeus did not create humankind, and he is not primarily concerned with their welfare."[13]

---

[12] Harriet R. Flower, *The Dancing Lares and the Serpent in the Garden: Religion at the Roman Street Corner* (Princeton, NJ: Princeton University Press, 2017); John Dominic Crossan, *The Gods of Ancient Rome* (New York: Harper, 2007).

[13] Mary Lefkovitz, "Greek Gods, Human Lives," New York Times (December 14, 2013).

Historically, no one hears the cry of the poor; no one remembers the voices of the oppressed. It is in the nature of poverty to be forgotten, walked past, to be unknown and easily dismissed. That is the way history has always dealt with the poor and suffering. They are not even backdrops to time and space. Their names are not remembered and their stories are not told. They are irrelevant to the politics of power and privilege that reign supreme in history's consciousness, that is until this moment when God intervenes and God enters history as a political agent.

We have heard the Exodus story often. We wonder whether we have domesticated it, softened its radical implications. Have we simplified it too much? Do we need to *feel* its implications and consequences more fully? We who have never been oppressed or under the thumb of any foreign power or raging army. We do not truly understand the numbness that comes over a people entangled in the conspiratorial networks of dictatorships. We do not really understand the Herods of history and the Pharaohs of Egypt, their tactics and their devices.

For example, however we wish to adjudicate the next steps that immigrants at our southern border should take and whatever are the fairest and most just policies we can apply, have we understood the meaning of their 2000-mile trek? Have we a sense of what might lie behind the decision for a mother or father to uproot their children from their homes and walk thousands of miles? What is that kind of desperation? What is that fear? What is that level of need?

Has anyone reading this book ever wanted anything that much? Has anyone ever yearned for something so desperately that they would go without food or water, without security or certainty, without past or future, in order to have a chance at a life in an unknown land, among the uninvited?

We do not often think about the situation of victims. We are not attuned to their cries or understand how easily they are dismissed or ignored in the traffic of modern life.

We need to be startled and shocked again by what Yahweh is doing. Gods do not intervene in time, except to further their own interests. In the ancient world, they could care less about the plight of the poor or the needs of the vulnerable. That a God, that *the* God of the Jews, had stepped into history, not on the side of the high and mighty, but on the side of the poor is beyond astounding. It is the turn of history.

Suddenly history is not simply tracking the mighty deeds of generals and armies, gods and emperors, the usual fare of religious narratives. History now becomes the narrative of the unknown and unwanted, the despised and dismissed. Yahweh walking onto the stage of human history, demanding a new outcome for the poor and staking the divine reputation on this outcome "to the thousandth generation," engages us in a new type of politics and a radically different understanding of religion. Religion has just gotten messy.

The gods will no longer be appeased by sacrifices. They will no longer be mollified and placated by virgins and child sacrifice. The gods, or at least the One who reigns from Jerusalem, will require justice and special attention to the widow and orphans. Faith will now be tracked on the margins of history, where Lazarus sits at the gate and the Jew lies thrown into the ditch.

Pharaoh resists the realization that he is not just on the wrong side of history. He refuses the conclusion that he is on the wrong side of God. What the Bible makes clear is that this is not an ordinary confrontation. (It never is – when God hears the cry of the poor.) All the imagery lines up to tell us that Pharaoh is up against God in a cosmic battle of good against evil where, before it is done, rivers will turn to blood, skies will choke with locusts, and plagues will fell all the playboys of Egypt.

We learn soon enough that it is not just not Pharaoh who has to let go of the Jews. The Jews have to let go of Pharaoh. That seems to be the hardest step of all. As the Scriptures demonstrate, the Jews do not want to let go of Pharaoh. Just a few miles down the road to freedom, they want to turn back to their predictable ways and their old routines. A few short puffs of liberation and they have already realized that freedom is hard and addiction is easy. However, God's word is clear – all our pharaohs must fall.

This is not just an ancient story. It is the grand narrative of all our struggles, because when we look deep into our own hearts, we have to admit that there are Pharaohs still ruling there that we do not want to give up. Maybe it is an abusive relative who gets on the phone and all she does is belittle us and we take it, call after call, year after year. Maybe it is an addicted child or a sibling who terrorizes with his guilty selfishness draining us of tears, money and even our will.

Maybe it is an old fear or anxiety inside our head, with the power of a Pharaoh, which convinces us that we will never be good enough, worthy enough or holy enough to succeed at anything really worthwhile.

We do not want to leave Pharaoh's side, because we have memories of the good old days, hot summer days on the banks of the Nile before the River had turned to bloody disappointments. We do not want to leave these Pharaohs because we have been in Egypt so long that we do not know what Eden feels like anymore. Our hard-hearted Pharaoh-friends have a way of making us doubt that there could be any more promised lands, new days, open opportunities, out there for us. Because of this, without any Eden to shoot for, our hearts turn as hard as Pharaoh's, until, out of the blue, we hear God's word to us – Go free. "I came that you might have life and have it to the full." (John 10:10)

God does not want us to have a half-life, broken days and unfulfilled nights. We were made for grace. God is coming in the Christ, always in the process of coming, to create a new heavens and a new earth. Jesus comes to split the water that separates us from our promised land, the land that stands on the other side of our pent-up fears and stored up suspicions.

The Recovery of Memory and Revitalization

As Christians, we have learned our doctrines well. They are deeply embedded in our mind. Those of us who grew up or were influenced by our highly defensive, apologetic age where every God-question required a sure and certain, a clear and distinct response (i.e. "why did God make me?"), we think that the recovery of memory is coming up with the right question and then the perfect answer.

Too many people who first came to me for therapy made the mistake in thinking that the way therapy worked was that they would come up with questions and I would provide answers. They would show me where it hurt (inside) and I would use my training and skills to provide an immediate psychological medication that would clear things up within a week or two.

They did not understand how pain or the psyche worked. They did not know nor appreciate that therapy, like conversion, has a lot to do with a recovery of memories with all their primal hopes and hurts.

To be authentic Christians, it is as if we must be first authentic Jews, in the sense that we must make the original memory of the slaves in the brickyards of Egypt our own. It must be ours not in the mind, where it can remain abstract and distant. It must become ours in the heart, in our feelings and in our gut. We must imagine what it is like to be in the brickyard, desperate and despised, hanging onto a belief in a God who has been silent and distant for generations. We must be the people who still cries in the night, hoping against hope, that this ancient God of a long-remembered covenant, might yet hear and act on our behalf.

The poet Kevin Covall tells of the hope that arises as their cries from the brickyards reach Yahweh and move Yahweh's Heart. He writes,

we needed inspiration, to be awakened
in our bodies, our lives made present
here we are
the world is not right, just or fair
the most have the least
the least have the most
all the pharaohs must fall
wake in this new day
let us live while we have the chance
while we have this day
to build and plot and devise
to create and make the world
just
this time for us
this time for all
this time the pharaohs must fall[14]

This time the Pharaohs must fall and we must hear the cries of the victims in the brickyards of Egypt. Our religion is meaningless without that habit of mind and heart. Our faith is nothing but magic without the history that overrides the blood and terror of the Pharaohs of every time and age. We need to hear the coming of the Lord, the One who has heard the victims' pleas and wishes to act in their favor and on their behalf.

Questions for Reflection

1. Chinnici reminds us that modernity forces us to forget our past in order to have a future filled with progress. What memories do we need to retrieve as a church?

2. As you think about your own personal history, what are your most cherished memories of God's rescue and liberation?

3. What personal or communal memories do you need to recover to deepen your experiences of empathy and sympathy?

4. What "Pharaohs" in your heart and mind must fall in order to have a more Christian or Franciscan life?

---

[14] Kevin Coval, "All the Pharaohs must fall" found at: http://kevincoval.com/kc/?p=1

Ricky's Story

We had arrived at the high school seminary together enthused to begin the long process of becoming priests. There were prayers to learn, rituals to perform, difficult studies to master, and a community to build. By the time I entered the seminary at the very tender age of 13, they were just beginning to go out of favor across the United States. There was nothing specific about the dissatisfaction. It was the first strains of a cultural disinterest in religious life and the first hints of a massive "vocational crisis" that would crest in the next two decades.

For our part, we were young, enthusiastic and passionate teenagers who wanted to follow Christ more deeply. We came to the seminary to learn how. As for myself, I compared the sacrifices of being far away from home, separated from friends and family, as part of the price that had to be paid for becoming the best priest I could be. I was like the young Olympic gymnasts who similarly traveled far from home and were separated from the ordinary dynamics of high school life in order to pursue a difficult goal. I strongly believed that I was following God's will for me, however unworthy I felt. The more than thirty young men who started with me were similarly devoted and energetic. We studied hard; we worked hard; our basketball and softball games were intensely competitive. We were in chapel six times a day, beginning at 5:40 am and ending at 8:40 pm. God was supposed to be our priority.

I was first exposed to sexual harassment and sexual abuse within a few short months of arriving. It unsettled me and left me profoundly confused. I was already naïve about sexuality as a thirteen-year-old. I had received the "basics" in grammar school, from family and a few friends before high school. Hormones among my group of buddies in eighth grade were high. There was a lot of sexual banter but it was always civil and under control.

Within a few months of freshman year at the seminary high school, I became a target of sexual harassment, although that language was nowhere in my vocabulary then. A small circle of boys had been gathering together for sexual play at night, in the dorms, after the priests all went to bed. No priests were ever involved and, throughout my seminary career, I never heard once of any priest abusing or harassing any of the seminarians. The harassment was coming from a few of my schoolmates and it was intense.

I was shocked and wanted no part of it. Mostly I was confused that this kind of behavior would erupt in a seminary context where it was made clear that any such behavior would not be tolerated.

My confusion deepened when one of the men in my class, Ricky, took me aside after a game of basketball and informed me that he was being "sexually abused," not by a priest and not by anyone on the staff of the high school. He was being abused by his grandfather and on a regular basis. One of the reasons he came to the seminary was to get away from the hurt, pain and shame, which he described quite intensely.

I had no categories as a thirteen-year-old in which to place or process this information. After all, I was very young and quite naïve. I was compassionate. I tried my best to express my empathy for my classmate and we resolved to get through this tough time together. I had no other skills or resources as a teenager. I had never heard of the sexual abuse of a minor and the thought of a grandparent abusing his grandson shocked and depressed me.

That event made me realize that I was holding on to way more than I could handle, stuff too difficult for me to process. I was afraid to go to the priests on staff. Honestly, I had never heard a priest talk about sex as far as I could remember. I didn't know how I would explain the incidents of sexual harassment that Ricky and I were experiencing. I certainly didn't want to implicate or "rat" on friends that I sincerely cared about. In short, I was lost.

I approached a member of the senior class that I knew to be a solid guy with good values and a warm heart. His maturity shone through from the first moment I told him about how I was feeling "overwhelmed" by the barrage of sexual requests I was getting and how shocked I was by them. He listened to me with mature compassion and, to this day, I am grateful for it.

He told me that he would intervene with the priest that we both knew was equally compassionate, with a healthy sense of what teen boys go through.

The priests took charge of the situation in a healthy and direct way. Nothing was swept under the carpet. Pastoral counseling sessions were begun immediately. Young men were provided with the help they needed to understand their sexual development and the importance of proper boundaries. The harassment stopped.

Ricky was the first person I knew who was sexually abused as a minor. His was the first voice of a victim that I heard. We never spoke again about his experience of abuse. The priests had taken charge of the whole situation and we processed our feelings with them, in confession and in spiritual direction. I presumed that Ricky had as well. I wondered whether I was a "good enough" friend to him after his difficult revelation. But I can't be sure.

Ricky left the seminary after that first year and returned home. I remember his voice to this day: the almost rote recounting of horrifying encounters with the grandfather he once loved, the monotone description of his feelings of disgust and self-loathing as if the events were all his fault and of his making. What struck me then, as it does now, is that Ricky seemed too shell-shocked by what happened to him to become enraged. There was a strange matter-of-fact quality to his recounting, as if it were all so very normal. It was indeed his normal.

There is greater awareness of sexual abuse today. There are tremendous resources for victims and those who help them. Back then, awareness was quite limited and most of us had no access to the kind of resources needed to recognize abuse and stop it.

Questions for Reflection

1. Who were the first people who told you about their abuse or shared an experience of prejudice, bias or structural inequality with you?

2. What do you remember of their voice: how did it sound to you then? How did you receive the sharing? How would you receive it now?

3. What resources are available to you now to recognize abuse and respond appropriately?

Chapter Three

We Hold the Death of the Lord

We are suggesting in this book that the renewal of Christian life is only possible through the recovery of the voices of victims, through the disruption of modernity's project to make us forget our painful past and its promises for an inevitable and unassailable human progress. Our deepest Christian memory, of course, lies in the Christ and our deepest memory as Franciscans lies in the One Francis knew as "Christ and Him Crucified." I want to meditate on the mystery and the meaning of the crucified Lord and what the recovery of that memory can be for us, as we search for ways to repent, recover and resurrect from these difficult days in the Church.

We start with our fundamental claim and starting point as Christians. One of my "go-to" expressions of this claim is found in David Haas' lyrics of "Now We Remain":

We hold the death of the Lord deep in our hearts.
Living, now we remain with Jesus, the Christ.

Once we were people afraid, lost in the night.
Then by your cross we were saved.
Dead became living, life from your giving.

Something which we have known,
something we've touched, what we have seen with our eyes:
this we have heard, life giving Word[1]

After more than two thousand years of Christianity, we know that we have an impressive history of scholarship, law, art, science and architecture. We have built a civilization that prizes and advances human dignity, the freedom of conscience, the belief in human progress and possibility, and we have a commitment to mercy and human rights

[1] David Haas, "Now We Remain," GIA Publications, 1983.

unparalleled by any other human project the world has undertaken. All of it flows from this memory of the death of the Lord, which we hold deep in our hearts. What is it that catches us and fascinates us about this figure in human history and this moment in human time?

Jesus is by all accounts the central figure of history for the past two thousand years. The question we must ask is – why? How did he become so prominent? What is it about his life, work, teaching, reputation, and death that have fascinated and preoccupied the minds of men and women for centuries?

At first glance, there is not much in his background that should catch our attention. He comes from the basically backwater and obscure town of Nazareth, in what was a politically and economically insignificant and occupied province of the Roman Empire. We know from the four Gospels written about him that he was a carpenter, a street preacher, and a healer with miraculous powers.

Jesus was not a priest, but a self-proclaimed prophet and teacher who got into trouble with both the political and religious authorities of his time. He was accused of treason by Rome and heresy by the highest Jewish authorities of his time. He was convicted in a stacked nighttime trial by the Sanhedrin and sentenced to death the next morning by the Roman governor in Jerusalem, Pontius Pilate. He suffered a horrific form of execution, being nailed to a cross on a Friday morning. He died from a slow form of asphyxiation and was buried in a borrowed empty tomb not far from Calvary, the execution site.

Soon after his death, there were reports that He was seen alive, first by his disciples and then by hundreds of witnesses with, as Thomas learned, the nail-marks in His hands, feet and side still clearly visible. His followers shared the conviction of a "resurrection from the dead."

During his short prophetic ministry, people spoke of him as "the Christ," the anointed one of God, the predicted Messiah. They pinned their hopes on him as the one who would finally reverse the sorry fortunes of Israel, the people of God who had suffered centuries-worth of foreign occupation, despite their claim and conviction of being God's "chosen people."

They were hoping for an eschatological transformation of Israel's situation ("the consolation") and a complete overthrow of Rome's control over God's chosen people. Jesus lived in a time of hot tempers and furious political rebellion. The mood was growing that the people had had enough of Rome and were anxiously awaiting a Messiah with the divine power and the political clout to throw Rome out of Israel once and for all, through violent means, if necessary.[2]

Even the language of John the Baptist was hot and violent. Remember that he speaks of God's axe being laid at the root of the tree, ready to cut down the state of infidelity (Luke 3:9). Jesus' response to the increasingly hot tempers of the time is decidedly non-violent. His repentance movement is long on mercy and compassion. Jesus believes that violent rebellion is a literal dead-end. Going up against Rome is self-defeating.[3] Jesus had seen and taken to heart how many recent "prophets" of Israel had ended up rotting on the crosses that were Rome's way of welcoming people to the city of Jerusalem, just in case anyone doubted who was in charge of the city.

For that reason, Jesus refused the political Messiahship the people were begging for and banking on, the forced rebellion against Rome, and the violent preoccupations erupting out of the frustrations of Israel. Jesus reminded His people, instead, that the poor were falling through the cracks created by the violent polarizations of the times in which they lived. He redirected their minds and hearts to mercy.

Jesus turned their attention to the victims of his time: Lazarus at the gate of the rich man (Luke 16:20), the Jew robbed and thrown into the ditch (Luke 10: 25-37), the prostitutes unable to be clean and righteous before the Law (Luke 7: 36-50). Somehow, for this messianic figure, hope does not emerge from the mighty hands of the victorious and the righteous. It is offered from the hands of the lowly, the left out and the left-behind. Jesus chooses another path of redemption that rejects rebellion and violent resistance.

The people's hopes and their claim of the Messiah's political arrival came to a screeching halt with his trial and execution. Jesus went from glory to shame, from fame to failure, from adulated to despised in a matter of hours. Treason and heresy should have signaled the end of all his prophetic claims. Jesus should have joined the long list of troublemakers who tried going up against the Roman Empire only to end up on the ash heap of history. And yet, his death turned into the central dividing line of history.

How did Jesus of Nazareth go from criminal to Christ? What is it about him that fascinates and intrigues? What is it that arouses the deepest spiritual emotions of the human heart and mind? What is the mystery that is "Jesus the Christ?"

---

[2] NT Wright, *Simply Jesus: A new vision of who He was, what He did, and why He matters* (New York: Harper Collins, 2011).

[3] NT Wright, *Jesus and the Victory of God* (Minneapolis: Fortress Press, 1996).

The Mystery of Jesus the Christ

Within a few years, this is what people were saying and praying about Him.

Let us give thanks to the Father
for having made you worthy
to share the lot of the saints in light.

He rescued us from the power of darkness
and brought us into the kingdom of His beloved Son.
Through Him we have redemption
the forgiveness of our sins.

He is the image of the invisible God,
the firstborn of all creatures.
In Him everything on earth was created,
things visible and invisible.

All were created through Him,
all were created for Him,
He is before all else that is,
In Him everything continues in being.

It is He who is head of the body, the Church.
He who is the beginning,
the first born of the dead,
so that primacy may be His in everything.

It pleased God to make absolute fullness reside in Him,
and, by means of Him, to reconcile everything in His person,
both on earth and in the heavens,
making peace by the blood of His cross.
(Colossians 1: 12-20).[4]

This hymn, which was being sung in small Christian communities in the Middle East, was already being remembered and passed around within twenty years of Jesus' death and resurrection. Many people who had known Jesus, walked with him, and seen him crucified would still

---

[4] The translation is from "The Liturgy of the Hours," (New York: Catholic Book Publishing Co., 1976).

have been alive when this hymn was being sung. Surely, the apostles would have still been alive. We know that Peter would not meet his own death for another decade. These eye-witnesses of Jesus' death would likely have heard the hymn.

The outlines of a new hope emerge shortly after Jesus' death and resurrection. Communities are singing a hymn of deliverance within the earshot of those trying to persecute and arrest them.[5] The hymn speaks of their experience of Jesus as one of rescue and liberation. The community sings of being released and delivered from some deep moral, religious and ethical ignorance and darkness. The hymn speaks of their experience as of immense importance not only for themselves but for the cosmos, as well. This is not a script of just personal reform or individual enlightenment. It is a cosmic event with personal and social meaning. Something utterly dramatic and transformative has happened in human history and the ones singing this hymn are its first witnesses.

The release and rescue they experience require a new obedience and commitment, as if they were being transferred from one sovereignty to another, from one time and kingdom to another. The text speaks of a relocation from a kingdom of darkness to a new kingdom of light. In that new place, they experience religious insight and an understanding of mysteries heretofore unknown or misunderstood. Truths once veiled in mystery and darkness are now revealed and seen in the open light of day.

In the transfer, one finds oneself under a new and compassionate authority, unlike the power of the Empire. A "beloved son" rules over this new kingdom of light. Time now belongs to Him. History is His. All power and all consolation emanate from Him. Those who have been rescued experience mercy, kindness and forgiveness from the Christ. They join together and become His "beloved community."

Those in the kingdom receive a "wisdom" that is distinctly different from every inherited philosophical and theological system to date. What they receive from the Beloved One is not some new ethical code or "superior" form of the world's ordinary knowledge. Theirs is a "wisdom" of another kind and order, which they accept as "a scandal to the Jews and nonsense to the Greeks" (1 Cor. 1:23). Their wisdom is not easily put back into old categories of thought. It is refreshingly new.

The hymn then goes on to describe who this Beloved Son is.

Jesus is acclaimed as "*the image of the invisible God*." According to Abraham Heschel, Jewish thought holds that the divine is largely silent and invisible – God is transcendent, mysterious, beyond human

---

[5] NT Wright, *Colossians and Philemon* (Tyndale New Testament Commentaries, Book 12) (Downers Grove, IL: IVP Publications, 2015).

comprehension and outside of human control.[6] This passage describes something quite different, however, about Jesus. He is within reach of humankind. The divine is made visible and accessible through Him. God is no longer concealed. Jesus is the departure from God's ordinary state of silence and aloofness. Jesus is a living experience of the transcendent Divine. Jesus is not like the prophets of old (i.e. Isaiah or Jeremiah) who simply speak for God or in God's voice. Jesus is not just an "interruption" of God. Jesus is the eruption of God in time and place. This hymn says something of Jesus that was never said of any of the prophets. He is the image, the reflection, the appearance and experience of God. Jesus makes visible what is invisible. Jesus reveals what has been concealed for all eternity.

The hymn goes on to say that Jesus is "*the firstborn of all creatures.*" As image of the invisible God, Jesus is also the image and reflection of humanity itself. Jesus is humanity's representative before God and is the representative for all creation, as well. Jesus' relationships are vertical and horizontal. As the image of the invisible God, Jesus holds a pre-eminence in the created world. Jesus has a kind of representative primacy over everything that exists.

One has to stop for a moment to take in the significance of what is being claimed here. The One named as image of the invisible God and as the pre-eminent firstborn of all creation is the same Jesus recently indicted, convicted and crucified on charges of treason and heresy by the highest civil and religious courts in the land. It is inconceivable that criminals of high treason and heresy would be remembered and lauded in such a manner during the very lifetime of those who had seen them tried, convicted and executed. And yet, this hymn vibrantly and confidently proclaims that Jesus has not only a unique relationship with the divine, it holds that He has *the* unique relationship to the divine and to all creation, as well.

Then, the hymn continues to make further statements that are as or even more outstanding. *"In Him everything on earth was created"* and *"all were created through Him,"* and "*all were created for Him.*" This text is not a science lesson. It is not providing a physical description of how created matter came to be. The hymn is not interested in molecular formulations or genetic permutations. It is a text about ontological meaning and purpose. The text tells us that, in some mysterious way, everything that exists was created *through* Him and *for* Him. Sun and moon, stars and

---

[6] Abraham Heschel writes, "As a rule, God is silent; His intention and design remain hidden from the mind of man," in Abraham Joshua Heschel, *The Prophets* (Peabody, MA: Hendrickson Publishers Marketing, 2014), 216.

seas, mountains and humankind all owe their existence, their coming into and sustenance in being, through the power of this Jesus of Nazareth.

The hymn presents the conviction among the early Christians that the Jesus who shared their history, their existence in time and space, shares history with all of creation, of every time and place. The beloved community that sings this hymn explodes with enthusiasm and passion. Theirs is a victory song that teases and inspires, leaving us to meditate on the pre-eminence and the primacy of the Christ over all in both the visible and invisible world. There is no one equal to Jesus; there is nothing that rivals Him. The text confidently proclaims that "*He is before all else that is.*"

To understand the passion of Western civilization over the past two thousand years, with its eruption of science and its affirmation of freedom, human dignity and human rights, one has to come to grips with the origins of this redemptive type of thinking. Our political and social theories are incomprehensible without it.

Although the notions of freedom, rescue and liberation outlined here have social and cultural consequences, they are not presented as a political construction. The text affirms freedom and liberation as religious constructs, derived from an understanding of the Christ. Their durability is tied to this figure, this person, who has the ability to transfer men and women from darkness to light and to relocate humankind from chaotic and dangerous relationships into the intimacy of the community of the beloved.

Western civilization after the death and resurrection of Jesus shows an astounding set of anthropological assurances: freedom over fate, enlightenment over ignorance, agency over apathy, opportunity over oppression, reason over superstition, and logic over magic. We see the tracks of these convictions in our law, science, art and architecture, and in our commitment to human rights, however imperfectly we have applied or been faithful to these convictions.

What has made these commitments durable is that they are highly personal. They are rooted in the Person of Jesus. He is the measure and the guarantor of their effectiveness. We have not inherited an abstract ethical code, an impersonal system of laws, or a complex superior teaching. Our redemption does not come from rules or doctrines. What we have is the experience of the living Christ, who dwells in our midst whenever two or three are gathered in His name. We abide in the experience of Christ, which is given as gift and grace.

In every time, generation, culture and era, we experience freedom, illumination, agency, reason, and logic by means of a power not our own.

We overcome ignorance, superstition and oppression of every sort by a grace that reconciles us to one another and to God by means of the "death of the Lord." Amazingly, the early church did not accept His death in its usual and expected narrative as political terror. Surely, it was all of that, fully all of that, and yet the community that sings of His dying receives it most profoundly as a pledge of peace, the social peace of Trinitarian relations over against ontological violence.[7]

A crucified death in the time and culture of Jesus was the ultimate sign of failure and religious rejection not only by the state but also by the divine. It was the ancient evidence of ignominy and shame. Notwithstanding that, the early church experienced Jesus' death in wholly other terms, as the testimony of the Father's incredible love for humankind and indeed for all creation. It was the supreme evidence of Jesus' enduring compassion across the ages. As scandal to the Jews and absurdity to the Greeks, it reveals a new wisdom of the humble God ready to divest God's self of all majesty for the sake of mercy.

The Recovery of our Memory: Simply Jesus

We have to pause and take a breath. The world is turned upside down; we are being shown and offered something unexpected and largely unrecognizable. We need to take a fresh look at what we are holding deep in our hearts, perhaps in the deepest and most hidden places of our souls. What we are holding is that our rescue and redemption happen in the experience of the Victimhood of Christ.

In his book, *Undergoing God*, the theologian James Alison makes the claim that our sacraments revolve around one central truth that Jesus is the Victim of history; we are not.[8] At the least, we are not victims in the deepest and truest sense that He is, for He alone is the Innocent One. He alone is the "spotless lamb" sacrificed and broken not for His offenses, but for ours. We do not go to our sufferings and our persecutions totally and fully innocent. As the Scripture says, "All have sinned and all are deprived of the glory of God" (Romans 3:23). What draws us to Christ is the innocence of His suffering and death, the trumped-up charges with their false accusations and their scapegoated conspiracies.[9]

---

[7] John Milbank, *Theology and Social Theory: Beyond Secular Reason* (Malden, MA: Blackwell Publishing, 1990).

[8] James Alison, *Undergoing God: Dispatches from the Scene of a Break-In* (London: Darton, Longman and Todd, 2006), 33-49.

[9] Rene Girard, *Things Hidden Since the Foundation of the World* (Stanford, CA: Stanford University Press, 1978).

What Jesus' death reveals is the way that evil operates; in it, we see how evil works. We see how easily, how effortlessly the innocent one is arrested, convicted, and crucified. We see in the Christ the fate of the innocent victims throughout history: the murder of Abel by Cain, the enslavement of the Jews in Egypt, the slaughter of the innocents in Bethlehem, and the execution of John the Baptist. There is a familiar ring to all these stories that resonates in our hearts, because we have all been there at one time or another in our lives.

We have been bullied and been the subject of rumors and gossip. We have been lied to and cheated on, stepped on and passed over, even if in some small way. We have been dissed and disrespected, betrayed by those we have loved and ignored by those we have cared about. We do not say these things to inflame our victimhood, for we know our own complicities. We know that we have participated in these self-same dynamics with others and about others.

The point I want to make is that we must hear the cries of the victims of history that emanate from Calvary. The sounds we hear from that place of the Skull are the accumulated cries of all those who have been victimized throughout history; from the sound of the slaves in the brickyards of Egypt to the cries of the 85,000 children who have died of starvation in the war of Saudi Arabia against Yemen today.[10]

On the Tuesday of the second week of Advent, we heard the provocative story from Jesus about the one lamb that was lost, the 99 sheep that remained, and the shepherd who goes in search of the lost one. (Luke 15:27). We had an open sharing of thoughts that day in the friary. My spontaneous sharing that day was that Jesus is both the good shepherd in the story who goes in search of the lost sheep outside the fold and he is, in a certain sense, the lost and abandoned lamb outside the circle of His people. He is the "stone rejected by the builders" who will become the cornerstone. On the Cross, he is the lost sheep, the abandoned lamb, outside the fold of the people of God. (Psalm 118:22; Matthew 21:42)

We need to feel the abandoned Christ, the lonely Christ, the rejected and solitary Christ, experiencing His abandonment as our own. For, as Scriptures say, "it was our infirmities that He bore, our stripes that He endured." (Isaiah 55:4; Matthew 8:17).

We must experience both sides of the mystery of the lost sheep. We must feel again the anguish of the lamb lost, apart and perhaps even abandoned by the ninety-nine, who do not care and cannot be bothered by the absence of the lamb. We must sit in that place of rejection, in

---

[10] Palko Karasz, "85,000 Children in Yemen may have died of starvation," *NY Times* (November 21, 2018).

that space of abandonment, that is the condition of far too many of our sisters and brothers stigmatized for their poverty, rejected because of their mental illness, all those who have become, what Bryan Massingale calls, "permissible victims" and the accepted collateral damage of our drive for profits at all cost. These are the "forgotten women and men" who become enraged by the injustice done to them, the unfairness inflicted upon them, outside the circle of opportunity, beyond the sheepfold of possibilities in our driven economy.[11] We must as Franciscans sit in that space of hot tempers and deep frustration.

We must also allow ourselves the opportunity to recognize the shepherd who comes to be with the lost sheep, first only to sit and calm the fears and anxieties, to listen to what it has been like for those abandoned and abused.

One might imagine the shepherd arriving on the scene and immediately scooping up the lost sheep, terrified and insecure—an American swat team approach to redemption. I do not imagine it that way. Perhaps it is my years as a therapist that lead me to conclude a more gentle and developmental approach. I imagine the shepherd arriving and simply sitting with the lost one and listening to what it has been like out in the cold, alone and afraid. Perhaps the shepherd listens with the lamb for the sounds of the night, for the howling winds of disappointment and frustration, before he takes the lamb into his arms to calm its anxious heart.

The shepherd listens, so that one day the lamb might sing with others in the fullness of empathy and solidarity –

Once we were people afraid, lost in the night.
Then by your cross we were saved.
Dead became living, life from your giving.

We hold the death of the Lord, deep in our hearts,
Living, now we remain with Jesus the Christ.

---

[11] Tommie Shelby, "Prisons of the Forgotten: Ghettos and Economic Injustice," in Tommie Shelby and Brandon M. Terry, *To Shape a New World: Essays on the Political Philosophy of Martin Luther King, Jr.* (Cambridge, MA: The Belknap Press of Harvard University Press, 2018), 187-204.

Questions for Reflection

1. In what ways have you experienced Jesus as rescue and liberation in your life?

2. Jesus gathers the voices of victims into His own voice as the Crucified. Who are today's victims of injustice? How is your community listening to and serving the victims of injustice?

3. Who are victims of injustice that your community should now consider serving?

Chapter Four

Francis as Crucified Victim and Prophet of Hope

For the past several years, ever since becoming Dean of the School of Franciscan Studies, Director of the Franciscan Institute, and Associate Professor of Theology and Franciscan Studies, I have had the privilege and the luxury to be immersed in Franciscan Studies. I have met and conversed with the greatest Franciscan theologians of our age. I have edited their books and articles. I get to review the classics of this period of the "*resourcement*" of Franciscan theology and I get to preview what Franciscan theologians are thinking about, musing about, getting excited about as they uncover new historical insights about Francis and the early Franciscan movement. It is such a long way from my meager introduction to Francis of Assisi when I was in novitiate. The Francis to whom I was introduced as an eighteen-year-old was the Francis of the pious stories and devotional images of the *Fioretti*. It was the uncomplicated, obedient and fully compliant churchman of the pre-Sabatier era, the Francis without culture and conflict, the Francis without drama or despair, the Francis without hysterics or history, more the plaster statue in the backyard than the religious genius and spiritual entrepreneur we know him to be today.

When I entered Capuchin life, sad to say, one could become a good Capuchin without knowing much about Francis of Assisi at all. Of course, we would read the Rule twice a week and the Testament of Francis on Fridays. We would study the Constitutions but we did so with a legal and canonical eye. We didn't have the tools, methods or even the interests then to study Francis as an historical figure (and a major one, at that). We knew almost nothing of what motivated him, the fears that preoccupied him, and the religious conflicts that emboldened him. The early friars, Hugolino, Honorius III, Lady Jacopa were simply liturgical props in the life of a saint.

It wasn't until the work of Franciscan scholars like Regis Armstrong, William Short, Dominic Monti, David Flood, Zachary Hayes and Wayne Hellman grabbed us by the throat and demanded our attention that we began to realize how engrossing, enticing, complicated and enriching Francis' life was.

I want to share with you what I have learned and what of it gives me immense hope for the revitalization of Franciscan life as we are about to close another decade of the 21st century. My premise is that we find the richest sources of hope in two moments of Francis' life: in his adolescent conversion and in his last sufferings before his death. Those two periods of Francis' life are rich sources for a renewed Franciscan spirit. Let us spend time with Francis – The Crucified Victim and Prophet of Hope.

Naked in the Public Square

When we first meet Francis before the bishop in the public square, he looks like a young man who is desperate and disillusioned. He is out of sorts with his family. His brother, Angelo, is convinced that he is out of his mind. He has been wracked by war, suffering most likely from what we would today diagnose as the deep spiritual and psychological wounds of post-traumatic stress disorder. A once jovial and popular adolescent, everyone's favorite "party-boy," who once believed he was made for glory, now wants off the social grid, so powerful is his disillusionment and disagreement with his family and his culture. On that day in 1206, as he stares into the eyes of the bishop and locks in on his father's fury and disappointment, he looks anything but hopeful. His journey to become the Prophet of Hope we know him now to be is a remarkable heroic tale.

Francis of Assisi (1182-1226) lived in a time of incredible violence and enormous greed.[1] The son of a wealthy cloth merchant, he lived the high-life and fast lane adolescence of an up and coming new generation of financial entrepreneurs. He was a walking advertisement for his father's fashion business and he was his father's promise for an economy based on hard work and merit not inheritance, as was the way of wealth in medieval times. He and his father were devoted to a new social ideal whereby families could work their way into the upper class and actually create status for those not born into privilege. Francis' father was tired of slogging his way back and forth to France to pursue his business, only to be interrupted and gouged by the endless tariffs and toll booths erected by noble families to keep them and no others in the privileged lifestyles to which they had become accustomed. Francis' father wanted to create a new model whereby people made money a new-fashioned way: they

---

[1] David B. Couturier, "Franciscan Economics in a Disenchanted World," *Franciscan Connections/The Cord* 65:3 (September, 2015), 41-43.

would earn it. It was a radical ideal that Francis and his father, Pietro, promoted and a dangerous one for the times in which they lived.

The medieval world knew almost nothing of "upward mobility," as we now know and suppose it. And the "majores" of Francis' day were not about to allow access to wealth that easily. The world, as they knew and wanted it, was designed for a hierarchy of the few above the many.

The tensions that developed in the 12th and 13th centuries around these questions of access and merit, privilege and power often turned deadly. It was a contest that Francis was at first willing to take up.

His adolescent dreams were of becoming a knight for the good and glory of Assisi. It was a dream that his father was only too willing to support. He outfitted Francis with the best military gear available. Francis, the playful darling of his friends, went to war with the blessing and the hopes of his family. However, something happened to Francis at the Battle of Collestrada, something that shook him to the core of his soul. Taken prisoner of war, he languished in prison for the better part of a year until ransomed by his father. He was never the same afterwards.

Like many soldiers before and after him, Francis had seen the fatal consequences of war. He had seen his friends, the ones he used to party with as minstrels on the streets of Assisi, now butchered on the bloody floor of the Umbrian Valley. Francis was deeply shaken by what he experienced. Francis would never pick up a sword again. However, Francis went further by questioning the roots of the violence and greed that had consumed his time and imagination. He understood something that many had missed in their justifications for violence in the name of privilege, namely that God was being implicated and even convicted by association with the greed of the day.

Francis had grown up on the apocalyptic and majestic images of God that were current in the Middle Ages. It was common belief that God looked after the world but on a throne and with a threatening glance and a thunderous judgment against evil. As a boy, Francis would have shaken with dread as he pondered the imperial character of the Almighty in his time. But something changed in his view of God after his experience of war. His well-chronicled conversion included not just sensitivity to the poor and a wondrous appreciation for the lowliest of creatures in nature. It also impelled Francis to a dramatic and radical love of the humble God, the naked divinity, and the approachable incarnate Christ of the Gospels, the One whose fundamental stance turned out to be mercy and compassion, and not angry judgment.

Francis came to the conviction that it was this tender and kind God that was obscured and defaced by the violence and greed of his world and its economic schemes. And so, it became Francis' mission to reveal once again the goodness of God, which was to be found in abundance in the lowliest and most vulnerable of creatures.[2] The logic of having by losing, getting by giving, pursuing light by dancing in the darkness, and claiming joy in the very collapse of sorrow was paradoxically enticing, the kind of twist in spiritual knowledge and action that only a *jongleur de Dieu* could perform. In the enigmatic way of mystics, Francis' "economy of abundance" was created by a poverty of dispossession.

Francis embarked on a new mission – to see and experience the world in the fullness of a God who was good, all good, supremely good, all the time and to everyone. And he discovered the remarkable principle that the way to experience the fullness of God was through a process of emptiness. That is, the way to enter the majesty of God was through experiences of minority. In order to experience the abundance of a good and gracious God, Francis had to open up new spaces emptied out of self-aggrandizement and competitive aggression. He had to find his way to the luxurious nature of God's kindness through the portals of vulnerability.

His contemporaries had proposed that the way towards God was through an imitation of majesty and the accumulation of power, prestige and privilege. Francis had learned just the opposite. The way to fullness was by emptiness. And, as his Franciscan brothers and sisters soon learned, this insight would have enormous impact for their use of money and their activities in the economic world. Their efforts to develop a fraternal or relational economy were not designed to reject or denigrate the world. They did not embark on poverty to castigate and bypass the natural world in order to "get to heaven" as quickly as possible. Quite the opposite!

Francis' re-thinking of the economics of his time, concentrated as it was on the development of his fraternity's use of goods and money, was aimed at the construction of security, joy and peaceful relations, elements of life sorely lacking in the culture of his time. Francis' rule was anticipating Christ's return to "create a new heavens and a new earth," by living in the simplicity of life that called on the brothers and sisters to live in communion and not in competition with one another. Francis wanted his fraternity to experience the fullness of God, not God's stinginess. And so, he created an economic model and plan of life that re-directed the brothers and sisters away from aggression and power-building.

---

[2] William B. Short, OFM, "What is the Franciscan Imagination," *Franciscan Connections/The Cord* 65:1 (March, 2015), 8-12.

The Early Origins of Franciscan Hope

Let's pull back from this now familiar story and ask ourselves what were the elements and early origins of Franciscan hope. What did the early Francis offer his brothers and sisters that gave them such hope for a better world and a repaired Church?

We know that the religious impulse of the people of Assisi was to build their hopes on the imitation of God's majesty. They had been offered the dream of accessing their rightful glory as citizens through the accumulation of new wealth circulating through Europe at the time. They would achieve their greatness through the concentration of power in the hands of a new entrepreneurial nobility, those who were willing to work hard enough at the new economy being built in Italy in the early days of the 13th century. This is the foundation of Francis' economic beliefs during his daring but playful adolescence.

In time, however, Francis saw through this ruse. He came to see clearly and personally what violence and greed had done to his own family; he saw the deadly effects on his young friends and neighbors at the Battle of Collestrada. He was horrified at the ease with which the elders of Assisi were willing to sacrifice the young and the poor to the machinery of war, all in the service of a lust for greed and violence. And so, he flipped the values, reversed the negative and asked the people of his generation not to pursue majesty but minority. He asked them not to scratch for the first place and highest rung of social standing. He challenged them to take the last and lowest place and to find their hope not in the assurances of politics and law, but in the simplicity of our often-overlooked original goodness.

On the back cover of my book on *Franciscans and their Finances: Economics in a Disenchanted World,* there is a quote from inside the book:

> Francis' fraternal economy is not primarily about dollars and cents, market shares or stock derivatives. It is about the destiny of men and women in the real world and how they come about a new security and peace in God. By the time his captivity as a prisoner of war had come to an end, Francis had given up on the violence and greed that fed the frenzy of Assisi. He found his peace in mercy – in the mercy that God had for him and in the mercy he could show to those who were poor and suffering. Francis gave away everything he had and felt the first taste of freedom in his whole life. He had given up on his need to climb and be right. He had let go of the desire to imitate majesty and

> control the world. He would never again have to go to war, because there was nothing that anyone else had that he wanted. There was nothing he had that he would not forfeit. He had Christ and Christ had him and that was enough for Francis to feel the "peace that passes all understanding."[3]

Francis now found his hope in the simplest and most unassuming places. He did not construct his hope anymore on what he needed to build, what he needed to gain, what he needed to do to be accepted and to be in grace with fortune and men's eyes, as Shakespeare might say.

Francis did not focus on scarcity, on what he yet needed to do and be, as we do in our culture. We live by an obsessive preoccupation that we never have enough and that we are never good enough, so that we need to have more and we need to be more.

Francis gave up that vacuous search for "more" and steadied himself with the gifts he already had all around him. He enjoyed, relished, and found delight in what was already there for his use in the world, in creation and in brotherhood.

Because he was secure in the knowledge that Christ had him and he had Christ, he asked for nothing more than what time and space already offered him. He had given up being anxious and fretful, as the Gospel advises us, and simply delighted in the moment, however it manifested itself to him.

Francis taught us to evangelize from the perspective of our gifts and not from our deficits. Chinnici reminds us of what that means:

> Practically speaking this means we need self-consciously and systematically to develop networks of communication designed to publicly enunciate our own gifts, to affirm each one's gifts, to create public spaces that serve to share our experience of giftedness from God with those whom we serve. We need to develop forms of speech that recall a communal memory of giftedness. We need to identify not the deficiencies in the world around us but its possibilities.[4]

We live in a time of extreme and damaging political discourse. It has become fashionable to ridicule, deride and demean anyone who disagrees with us and to lie publicly and brazenly, whenever wished or

---

[3] David B. Couturier, *Franciscans and their Finances: Economics in a Disenchanted World* (St. Bonaventure, NY: Franciscan Institute Publications, 2017).

[4] Joseph. P. Chinnici, "Passing on the Seal of Franciscan Life," *Franciscan Connections/The Cord* 68:4 (Winter, 2018), 14.

needed. If it serves our ends, any and all means are now justified. The French philosopher, Pierre Manent, calls this the "fecundity of evil," the Machiavellian notion that, in the realm of politics and economics, we should no longer strive after the good.[5] Goodness is too unstable and insecure to be the foundation of politics and economics. As I have previously noted, under this scheme, "nature and grace can no longer found humanity's progress in a world constructed for self-sufficiency and individual determination."[6] "The best we can do… is to use violence, fear and competitive aggression to our advantage. We need to use evil to create a common good." [7]

Francis would disagree. It is time for a new awareness of grace and gifts already among us. There are two attitudes that are required for this to happen: (1) a return to a real spirit of "*sine proprio*" and (2) a return to a spirit of reconciliation.

Sine Proprio and the Dispossession of the Heart

Francis of Assisi saw the dead-end of a culture and an economy based on the twin dynamics of violence and greed. He once said that he didn't want stuff because he didn't want to have to defend that stuff at the end of a sword. He had seen and experienced too much of the violent underside of his own father's greed and his society's craving for revenge. And so, Francis decided to live a life of "*sine proprio*," with "nothing of his own," where he would simply use, not own, the goods of this earth. By not owning things, he would not be tempted to dominate, deprive or domesticate his brothers and sisters by any trick of hierarchy or superiority.

In developing a new fraternity built on the grounds of "*sine proprio*," Francis took himself and his brothers out of the dynamic of inevitable violence that trapped Assisi and its surrounding cities. Because Francis and his brothers owned nothing, they had nothing to protect and they had no reason to go to war. Francis used to say often that the only thing we really own are our own sins.

Francis invites us to de-clutter our souls in four ways:

---

[5] Pierre Manent. "Machiavelli and the Fecundity of Evil." Chap. 2 in *An Intellectual History of Liberalism*. Translated by Rebecca Balinski. (Princeton: Princeton University Press, 1995).

[6] Couturier, *Franciscans and Finances*, x.

[7] Ibid.

- Return to your deeper and truer desires. Get behind and beyond the fabricated and insecure desires of the marketplace. Find the truth, beauty and goodness you're looking for in God.

- Divest yourself of all that obscures your clear view and ready access to God, yourself, your world and everything in it. Release yourself from the fog and frenzy of consumerism. Learn to live with what you need and re-learn what it means to share.

- Treat the world and everything in it gently. We have been so trained to enter spaces with suspicion, competition and aggression. We need re-think our initial encounter with the world and with ourselves, the one person with whom we can be harshest of all. We should greet everyone with a merciful social imagination of "*pax et bonum*" (peace and all good).

- We should stop playing the part of victim and victimizer that we have been assigned in the commercial liturgy of the consumer-based society.[8] Let me explain.

The theological and psychological logic of "*sine proprio*" is profound. Francis arrived at this theory of "*sine proprio*" by meditating on the coming of the Christ and the poverty of His Incarnation. The Word of God, through whom and for whom all things are created, came to this world with nothing and died on the Cross with nothing. And bringing the realization of this (and his own) poverty to prayer and to liturgy taught Francis another profound lesson, i.e., that ultimately, we are not the victims in this world.

Once again using the insights of theologian James Alison, we learn how the liturgy revolves around one truth and that is that *we* are not the victims of the universe. Because of our sins, however great or small they may be, we are always victimizers and perpetrators; we are always sinful. Christ, on the other hand, is the only true Victim and the One Sacrifice, poured out and given out once and for all.[9]

Clutter exists to fill in the spaces, to cover the cracks, to disguise the holes in our armored security and armed surety that we have been done wrong and need a never-ending supply of consolations. Advertisers and

---

[8] A mosaic-age Capuchin friar, Erik Lenhart, finds correspondence between the first three steps and St. Bonaventure's three levels of the spiritual life: purgation, illumination and union. I thank him for this insight.

[9] James Alison, *Undergoing God: Dispatches from the Scene of a Break-In* (London: Darton, Longman and Todd, 2006), 33-49.

marketers are banking on every insecurity they can uncover so as to hawk a product that will serve as a palliative and somehow demonstrate that we have gotten over our fears and conquered our insecurities, after we have sprayed "Eternity," worn J Brand's "Refuge" or carried Judith Leiber's "New Long Kiss" clutch bag from Nordstrom's.

Knowing how violence and greed were connected to stuff, how this dynamic obscured the experience of a good and gracious God and how it endangered the peace of his world, St. Francis refused to play the part of the victim or victimizer in a greedy world. He would no longer be the victimizer who had to have more to prove himself and he would no longer be the victim who needed more to find himself.

In this way, he created a group of brothers and sisters in fraternities of mutual donation not competition. He created a new economy, a fraternal economy, where stuff is limited to the "minimum necessary not the maximum allowed."

Francis went so far as to refuse his brothers permission even to touch a coin. He did so because in his day coins were the means by which men and women were judged in society and before God. A person was only as worthy as the stack of coins he/she carried. Francis refused to allow his brothers and sisters to be put on such an insecure and imprecise scale. No coin, he believed, could capture the ineffable mystery and awesome dignity of each and every individual, however limited or financially poor they might be. Francis would not allow coins or clutter to obscure, invalidate or minimize the goodness of God he saw in people.

Sine proprio is the ultimate act of the dispossession of the heart. It is the final surrender of the human spirit that will not seek to dominate or deprive anyone for one's own autonomy, sovereignty or majesty. It is as if Francis is saying -- I will not try to own my brothers or control them. I will not try to control the Order and shape it according to my wishes and needs. I will not begin any discussion from the rickety and insecure framework of deficit thinking and scarcity-mindedness. I will train myself to be attentive to the goodness of God displayed by the grace of God in the gifts of creation and brotherhood.

But, it is on Mount LaVerna that Francis finally seals his own life and mission. He has struggled mightily for the past several years with sickness, pain, disillusionment and isolation as he nears his own death. He goes to LaVerna to find faith, hope, and love again.[10]

---

[10] Joseph P. Chinnici, "Passing on the Seal of Franciscan Life," *Franciscan Connections/The Cord* 68:4 (Winter, 2018), 4-21.

La Verna and the Hope of a Reconciled Humanity

By the time Francis comes to La Verna at the end of his life, he is broken and disillusioned, once again. He has come back from his meeting with the Sultan at Damietta severely ill and broken-hearted at the developments in the Order. He has given up authority as Minister General of the Order but, as Jacques Dalarun writes so chillingly and convincingly, he is ambivalent over the paradoxes of power that he still wishes to wield on the brotherhood.[11] He is convinced that he has failed and his movement is being destroyed. His eyesight is failing and his vision of a hopeful future is severely clouded by his depression and anxiety.

At the beginning of his conversion, Francis prayed:

Most High, glorious God,
Enlighten the darkness of my heart,
And give me True Faith,
Certain Hope, Perfect charity,
Sense and knowledge,
Lord that I may carry out
Your Holy and True Command.[12]

Now, at the end of his life, Chinnici reminds us, Francis faces his weak faith, his fragile hope and his imperfect love. He comes to La Verna in deep distress. It is not simply that the brothers do not trust him; they don't. It is not only that the brothers are tired of him; they are. His distress is deeper. As Chinnici once again tells us,

> His experience has taught him that coming to God through creatures is good but not sufficient. In times of difficulty the eye of the mind can be blind and the affections can grow cold. The world no longer shines with "glory" (Is 6:3) and "sweetness." The Church, whose sacramentality has been so evident in the past and now whose authorities have caused him harm, no longer reveals the Gospel with sufficient luster to light his way. His brothers, except for a few friends, have clouded the horizon of God's call and what up to that time had been his own zealous

[11] Jacques Dalarun, *Francis of Assisi and Power* (St. Bonaventure, NY: Franciscan Institute Publications, 2007).

[12] St. Francis of Assisi, *Prayer before the Crucifix.*

> project. The world around him no longer serves sufficiently as a mediator of faith, hope and love.[13]

Chinnici reminds us that Francis came back to the questions posed at the very beginning of his conversion, before he embraced the leper – how can he love the unlovable? In whom can he place his faith? From where can he find a renewed hope?

We can relate to the awesome power of these questions, we who have seen too many scandals, suffered through too many betrayals, and endured too many disappointments. We too now have to find a way to a more durable faith, hope and love. We cannot rely anymore on youthful passion. The glory of our early days in the Order have been tarnished; the enthusiasms of our younger days in the Church have been weathered and, despite our best efforts, life makes it hard to come by a durable hope.

What happens to Francis in the midst of his deteriorating faith is a graced affirmation. When he was young and in deep distress and profound disillusionment, Francis heard the voice of a crucified young man who told him to pursue an action of purification. The voice from the Cross at San Damiano propelled Francis to repair the church.

Now at a time of deeper distress and more profound physical and moral suffering, Francis once again sees the crucified. It is the vision of the Seraph. Francis understands the significance of what is being revealed to him. Francis has experienced the last several years as a failure of his call and mission. He has lost control of the Order that the Lord had given him. However, what he experiences on La Verna is an affirmation filled with the personal love of Christ for him. Francis sees once again that it is the humanity of the Christ that saves, the humble Christ who redeems. It is the pierced and crucified seraph who rescues and releases the world. The "image of the invisible God" is the crucified Victim. Francis learns from this that, as it is for the Christ, so it is for him. It is his humanity, in all its weakness, that serves the cause of the Lord.[14] The seraph is not only an image of the Christ, it is also a mirror image of Francis himself. Francis is now the crucified victim who becomes the prophet of hope. What the seraph is, Francis has become.

This experience now buoys Francis. He composes his "*Canticle of the Creatures*" and is reconciled, in gratitude for the generosity of God.[15] He finds his way through weakness to true faith, certain hope and perfect charity. He now knows that it is not his faith, hope and love for God that

---

[13] Chinnici, 16.

[14] Chinnici, 16.

[15] Jacques Dalarun, *The Canticle of Brother Sun: Francis of Assisi Reconciled.* Philip Yates, trans. (St. Bonaventure, NY: Franciscan Institute Publications, 2016).

matter most. It is the faith, hope and love that God has in him![16] Francis had come to La Verna hoping for consolation; he has received affirmation instead. His life of poverty and minority, of mercy and compassion, *sine proprio,* has not been in vain. Francis has received a foretaste of heaven and exults in it.

Francis' campaign of renewal has not been won by structural adjustments or legal maneuvers. Francis went to La Verna and heard the Voice of the Victim once again, the seraph of love in crucified form. Francis had to plunge himself deeply into the wounds of the Christ in order to understand his own history. There are no guilty bystanders in this drama. There are only active participants. There is something more than sympathy, empathy and lament going on. On La Verna, Francis becomes the victim whose voice he first heard from the Cross at San Damiano. The "vox victimarum" of La Verna becomes the "*Canticle of the Creatures*" that Francis composes soon thereafter, in which he exults in the beauty of God in the sun and the moon, in flowers and stars, as sisters and brothers.

It is only as the crucified victim that Francis can trust, hope and love again.

> He can now trust again because the One who is most High has trust in him; he can hope because the One who is most powerful has hope for him; he can now love because the One who is all good invites him into loving. He has discovered once again the presence of a God who comes to him in the condition of being human. And in this experience, he can accept his own diminishment as a pathway through which he comes to belong to God.[17]

Francis is victim not above or by the side of all other victims in history. He sees and knows himself as victim in the Victim who is the Christ. He becomes the victim because he has taken into himself the horrors, the trauma and the fullness of pain that all victims experience. He takes on the weakness of his brothers, their callous rejection of him and their early inspiration. He is the leper now embraced by the Christ. As a crucified victim in the Christ, he now can embrace the world and all its creatures with a grace-filled exultation in the mercy and kindness of God.

---

[16] Chinnici, 16.

[17] Ibid, 17.

Conclusion

The take-away from La Verna at the end of his life is profound and unexpectedly hopeful. Francis approaches the fragility of humankind, its weaknesses, limitations and sinfulness, not from the perspective of his own well-worn humility, but from God's. Francis has come to the limits of his humility, but not God's. Francis now knows that there is no other path by which to enter into the presence of God, except through the portal of human weakness and God's crucified humility.

Francis has identified with the leper; he has united himself with the brothers; he has drawn bonds of fraternity with the Sultan and indeed with all creation. Now from the perch of La Verna, he is taught how to see the world fully from God's perspective, from deep within the crucified humility of God, from the unfathomable well of God's profound mercy. He had come to the dead end of his own powers to be gracious and merciful, forgiving and compassionate and now Francis learns to rely solely and completely on Christ's power in him. "It is now no longer I who live, but Christ who lives in me," is how St. Paul says it in Galatians.

What inspires Francis now is that he can see clearly and feel intensely what God is doing through his fragility, through the friars' indifference, and through his own bodily diminishment and weakened state. God is revealing God's true self, God's compassion and kindness, through the intensity of all that is weak and broken in us. Francis does not offer laments for victims. Francis doesn't offer them his empathy or sympathy. Francis enters their pain. He hears their voice so intensely and fully, without defense or protection, that he becomes the victim in the pain of the stigmata. As a crucified victim, he experiences the overwhelming love of God for the lost and broken ones of the world. He experiences in himself the love that God has for him and the whole world. That is why Francis can now honestly and exultantly exclaim the universal fraternity of all creation.

Questions for Reflection

1. At the end of his life, Francis came to the limits of his own humility and had to rely on the humility of God for inspiration and strength. What are your own personal limit-points that God may be using for good?

2. In what ways does the example of Francis open up new pathways for hope in this time of church crisis? How could the church renew itself through humility and minority?

Chapter Five

Clare the Proto-Feminist of Hope

It's been twenty-five years since the publication of Margaret Carney's book, *The First Franciscan Woman: Clare of Assisi and her Form of Life.*[1] It deserves a hearing and a read from Franciscan brothers and sisters, since it revolutionized the way that the English-speaking world understood Clare as a founder in the Franciscan movement, with a mind of her own and a vision with her own unique Franciscan stamp on it. The book makes the convincing case that Clare was a strong and decisive leader on her own terms, inspired by but not restricted to Francis' formula.

Having completed her MA at Duquesne University and another MA in Franciscan Studies at St. Bonaventure University, she earned her doctorate with a specialization in Franciscan spiritual theology from the Pontifical Antonianum University in Rome. With those credentials, she joined a small band of European and American scholars pursuing a new look at Clare of Assisi, people like Marco Bartoli, Maria Pia Alberzoni, Jean-Francois Godet-Calogeras and Regis Armstrong, to name just a few. Research was showing that Clare was more than a submissive seedling planted under Francis' protective shade. She was a strong woman in her own right, who spent twenty-seven years after the death of Francis, developing her Franciscan form of life against difficult clerical odds, positing a feminine form of governance that was unique for the time in which she lived. As Carney concludes:

> We must establish Clare in her rightful place as a threshold figure among medieval women of spirit. She was the first woman to write a Rule sanctioned with pontifical approval. She dared to synthesize the evangelical ideals of Francis, the new forms of urban religiosity, and the best wisdom of the monastic tradition to create a new and enduring order in the Church. She testified to Francis not only by the humility of her faithfulness, but by the authority of her leadership and formative ministry. She stands

[1] Published by Quincy University's Franciscan Press in 1993.

> before us today still serving as "instruction and a lesson to others who learned the rule of living in this book of life." (Rev. 21:27) (Bull of Canonization, 10).[2]

Re-reading this book now twenty-five years on, one wonders – how did we ever miss Clare's significance as a leader in her own right? How did we not gauge the radical nature of her spiritual impulses and not reverence her subversive acts to create a hard form of absolute poverty to convince the world that women were just as strong as, if not stronger than, men and thus must be allowed to follow Christ not at a submissive distance, but up front and full-throated. How did we not reverence Clare sooner as the mother of intentional discipleship!

We should have noticed this from the moment Clare engineers her escape from the noble class in which she was born, walks through "the door of death" in the middle of Palm Sunday night and meets Francis near the Porziuncula, where she receives her tonsure and becomes the first woman in the Franciscan movement.

It was a profoundly difficult maneuver and the act itself shows this eighteen-year old's amazing courage and fierce determination to be all that Francis was but in a uniquely feminine form. We have in our possession eyewitness accounts of that Palm Sunday night from the proceedings of her canonization. They tell a gripping tale of spiritual release.

> After the news reached her relatives, they condemned with a broken heart the deed and proposal of the virgin and, banding together as one, they ran to the place, attempting to obtain what they could not. They employed violent force, poisonous advice, and flattering promises, persuading her to give up such a worthless deed that was unbecoming to her class and without precedent in her family. But, taking hold of the altar cloths, she bared her tonsured head, maintaining that she would in no way be torn away from the service of Christ. With the increasing violence of her relatives, her spirit grew and her love-provoked by injuries-provided strength. So, for many days, even though she endured an obstacle in the way of the Lord and her own [relatives] opposed her proposal of holiness, her spirit did not crumble and her fervor did not diminish. Instead,

[2] Margaret Carney, *The First Franciscan Woman: Clare of Assisi and her Form of Life* (Quincy, IL: Franciscan Press, 1993), 19.

amid words and deeds of hatred, she molded her spirit anew
in hope until her relatives, turning back were quiet.[3]

Clare extracts herself from the domestic and protected life that nobility required of her. She refuses to follow the script of women in the Middle Ages that required women to be spoken for, curfewed, and accompanied. She refused to be bound by the gender norms of an arranged marriage and so she released herself to take on the total freedom of absolute poverty.

She had seen and heard Francis of Assisi from the window of her room that overlooked the square in front of the Cathedral of San Ruffino, where Francis often preached. It has been long held that she went searching for Francis, but historical research now tells us that it was Francis who went in search of the Lady Clare. He had heard of her holiness; he had listened to stories of her service to and love for the poor already at the tender age of sixteen. Clare's holiness, goodness and compassion were well known throughout Assisi. Francis wanted to meet her.

They met in secret because her family would never have allowed her access to the strange son of Pietro Bernardone. As nobles they already had experiences of the Bernardones' strange plots to overthrow the noble class and establish the merchant class as a new form of entrepreneurial nobility in Assisi. Clare's family already had to escape for their lives to Perugia when the merchants of Assisi fomented an armed rebellion to overtake control of city government. No. They would not have allowed Clare access to this delusional son of their sworn enemy. They were concerned enough with Clare's resistance to an arranged marriage, a polite and civil gesture that would solidify the family's standing in the city and secure her inheritance for future use.

By the time Clare got to Francis and had received her tonsure, she had already given away her fortune to the poor no less. This was a gesture that her relatives could not stomach. As one of three girls, with no male heirs, the women had some control over their fortune but the men were used to steering women in the right direction, in the way the men wanted the women to act. Clare had other ideas.

She wanted to follow Francis and his way of absolute poverty, without limit and with no restrictions or special conditions because she was a woman. If men had to sell all that they had and give it to the poor, this is what Clare would do. The men in the family might have

---

[3] *The Legend of Clare, CA:ED, 287* accessed at: https://www.franciscantradition.org/clare-of-assisi-early-documents/legend-of-saint-clare/464-ca-ed-1-page-287.

tolerated Clare joining a local abbey where her money could be held in a dowry in case she ever left the abbey and returned to her senses. But now, the money was gone. The land she owned was sold off and the money given to the poor, a humiliating gesture, for sure.

For her protection, Francis brought Clare to the Benedictine Sisters at San Paolo della Abbadesse. The abbey was under the protection of Bishop Guido of Assisi, who had to be in on the plot to spirit Clare out of town. She had to go through the gate that the bishop's guard protected and only the bishop could have ordered the guard to let her pass unaccompanied at night.

She stayed there eight days, working as a servant. Clare did not like it. She did not want to be a monastic nun. She wanted Francis' lifestyle of absolute poverty and service. The monastery was under the Bishop's jurisdiction. In 1198, Pope Innocent III issued a ruling prohibiting under pain of excommunication anyone using violence there who was not acting on behalf of the bishop. It was Francis' intention to keep Clare safe there, at least for a short while.

However, the nuns did not want trouble with Clare's rich and powerful family. The family came to get her; there was some violence, but Clare invoked the right to sanctuary by holding onto the altar cloths. The family abandoned their quest to bring her home because of her own "unconquerable perseverance." They were stunned when Clare showed them her tonsure, a formal act of "being in religion."

Her sister, Beatrice, reveals that Clare sold her entire inheritance and gave the money to the poor. Clare and her sisters had the family inheritance: not just money, but property. Her relatives wanted that property. They wanted to buy Clare out. She believed the money belonged to the poor. Therefore, she would not give it to a religious community, as the Benedictines would. She would not hold onto it, in case her religious life didn't work out. She sold the property outright and gave all of the money to the poor.

To make matters even worse, sixteen days after Clare's conversion, her sister, Catherine (later Agnes) follows Clare. "Twelve men, burning with anger and hiding outwardly their evil intent, ran to the place and pretended to make a peaceful entrance." Here is how the scene went down:

> Led by Agnes's and Clare's paternal Uncle Monaldo, the men had already given up on retrieving Clare. When Agnes refused to go with them, they seized her. The Legend graphically describes the men's violence against the young girl. They

> were perhaps emboldened because San Angelo lacked the papal protections granted to San Paolo. "One of the knights in a fierce mood ran toward [Agnes] and, without sparing blows and kicks, tried to drag her away by her hair, while the others pushed her and lifted her in their arms." This is probably one of the seven knights who the witness Pietro had said resided in Clare's home. Agnes screamed to Clare for help. "While the violent robbers were dragging the young girl along the slope of the mountain, ripping her clothes and strewing the path with the hair [they had] torn out, Clare prostrated herself in prayer with tears." Then God miraculously intervened: Agnes became too heavy to carry. Other men ran from nearby fields to help the group absconding with Agnes, but her body could not be budged. This elicited further violence: Agnes's enraged uncle raised his hand to strike her dead, but was stymied when his hand was itself struck with an excruciating incapacitating pain. Predictably, an unqualified victory concludes the story. When Clare approached and asked her relatives to desist, they bitterly abandoned the near-dead sister, and she arose, rejoicing that she could devote the rest of her life to God. Notably, Francis, too, makes an appearance in the story: he tonsures Agnes and, with Clare, teaches her about the Lord's path. Like Clare, Agnes was received into religious life by Francis himself. [4]

Why were the men so angry? They were losing both Clare and Agnes' inheritance and family property. Matters would only "get worse" for them. Eventually, Clare's mother, Ortulana, would join Clare's community, as would Clare's sister, Beatrice, some eighteen years later.

CLARE'S LIFE AS A LESSER SISTER

Clare survived Francis by twenty-seven years. In many ways and against multiple odds, she held firmly to the primitive ideals of Francis, even under the unfair and unintended monastic life that the Church forced on her. Never one to brood and always one to act, Clare shaped and formed her community of women into a distinctly Franciscan expression. It was not easy. Most of the friars wanted no part in taking care of the sisters. Hugolino as Cardinal and then

---

[4] Catherine M. Mooney, *Clare of Assisi and the Thirteenth-Century Church: Religious Women, Rules, and Resistance* (Philadelphia: University of Pennsylvania Press, 2016), 24.

as Pope tried diligently to force Clare and her sisters into his own monastic community of women. Clare would not have it. She was not a follower of Hugolino, whether he was a cardinal or a Pope. She had left home to follow Francis and she would do so to her dying day.

Clare's Life at San Damiano

Soon after her conversion and after a very short and unpleasant stint at the Benedictine Abbey, probably because Francis and his brothers had not yet completed the renovations needed on the building of San Damiano, Clare took up residence at San Damiano. It was named after Damian, the patron saint of healers. It was a hospice for the poor and probably contained within its walls a hospital for lepers and the most vulnerable of society, those already rejected and dismissed in the town above them.

It was here that the "Poor Ladies" took up their residence and tried to live the same lifestyle as the "Lesser Brothers." These "little sisters" had the grit and determination to want to live the Gospel as fully, as completely, as austerely and as poorly as the men. They were not going to be confined and constricted by their gender. Their motivation had to do with as complete an imitation and as direct a following of the incarnate Jesus, the man of the Gospels, as possible. They read the Gospels without gloss. They did not see the hierarchical differentiations that had accumulated over time; they did not notice in the Gospels any of the cultural and class-based stratifications that had accrued within their own cultural context. They only heard the simple command of the Lord to "come follow me!"

The "Lesser Sisters" saw this as addressed as equally and as forcefully to them as it was to the men of their time. They would not accept nor would they follow any advice or command that would cheapen, lessen, or belittle their call as equal members of the Franciscan movement. In this way, we see evidence of Clare's original determination and her radical commitment to feminine equality, unheard of in the times in which she lived. We see this determination and courage in clear light, already at the age of eighteen. She manages, directs and undertakes her conversion from noblewoman to poor lady, from the social onlooker at the castle window overlooking the village square near the Cathedral of San Ruffino to the woman in charge at the hospice filled with lepers in the valley below.

Clare's fastings demonstrated her fierce determination to be as strong in the faith as her male counterparts. She fasted on Mondays, Wednesdays and Fridays and it was a complete fast, until Francis, with his ever-present merciful disposition, asked Clare to modify her fast for the sake of her health. She did. On her fast days, she resorted to eating a half of a roll.

It is unclear whether at the beginning the Lesser Sisters had external ministries like those of the friars. The 1216 letter from Bishop Jacques de Vitry who makes one of the first public notices of the activities of what he witnessed of the "Lesser Brothers and Lesser Sisters" suggests some equal and common sharing of tasks, especially among the poor and in the hospice of San Damiano. We know that activities will change under the influence of the Cardinal-Protector of the Franciscan Movement, Cardinal Hugolino, later Pope Gregory IX. The intention at the beginning, at least in the mind of Clare, was anything the friars could do as "lesser brothers," she and the sisters were determined to do with equal fervor, passion and strength. It is clear that the men found this level of equal determination and equal strength hard to bear.

Clearly, women, at the time of Francis and in the minds of most men in society and in the church, were called to follow Christ in poverty, chastity and obedience. At the same time, certain protections were thought to be needed to make accommodations for their "weaker sex," their more "limited" abilities and their more "delicate" dispositions. In acts that can surely designate her as the "proto-feminist" of the woman's equality movement of the 20th and 21st centuries, Clare firmly, decisively, courageously, and counter-culturally rejected these assumptions in the most forceful of ways.

Hugolino, both as Cardinal and as Pope, tried to protect Clare and her sisters from their passion for poverty and a direct reading of the Gospel for feminine disciples. One need not paint negative aspersions on Hugolino. He was as trapped in his cultural and gender biases as any of the smartest and holiest men of his time. Clare would have to fight him constantly and consistently throughout his reign, since he clearly did not understand or agree with her conviction that women could be as strong disciples of the Lord as men. Women could follow Francis as poorly and as austerely as men could. She would be the first and most assertive of Francis' lesser sisters, demonstrating by her work, her ministry to the sick, her deep devotion to prayer and Eucharist, and by her fasting how much she wanted to be identified with the crucified One, in love with the world and indeed with all creation.

Her convictions about the power of women became popular. By 1212, five women had entered the community. By 1220, the community grew to 12 or 13. Soon her communities would be filled with relatives—her mother, sisters and cousins—and with other rich women of the area who also wanted to give up their riches for a more direct and compassionate following of the Lord. This was not a life where any of them would be pampered, waited on, or taken care of. Those days of being spoken for, protected, and directed by men were over.

The Lesser Sisters were learning to create their own feminine approach to the divine. In lieu of the hierarchies of grace and ritual to which the church was accustomed, Clare and her sisters created a governance of mutual charity, one designed for collaboration, discussion and shared decision-making. They spent their work hours spinning corporals and altar linens, working (some for the first time) in gardens with their own hands, only relying on the friars help when they simply did not have enough to eat.

Hugolino and Clare

Hugolino was designated the "protector of the Franciscan movement." He was close to Francis and he was an earlier admirer of Clare's holiness. Although a high-ranking canon lawyer and cleric, he was a great supporter of religious life and worked tirelessly for its renewal. One of his dreams was to bring order and stability to all the penitential movements arising throughout Europe, especially among women. To that end, he unified disparate women's communities, each with diverse rules, customs, procedures, and ways of serving, and tried to unite them into one complete and ordered community, under a rule that he wrote and an Order that he would supervise, which he first named "The Order of Penitents." In time, he would name it "The Order of San Damiano," banking on the name and popularity of the woman who oversaw the work of the community established at "San Damiano," Clare of Assisi.

Clare was not of the mind of joining Hugolino's movement or of abiding by its structures or constrictions. Hugolino wanted an order of nuns. Clare saw her women as "sisters." Hugolino wanted all the women in his Order to be "cloistered," hidden away from the ways and cares of the world. Clare, on the other hand, hoped for a lifestyle similar to that of Francis and his lesser brothers. She wanted a women's community of itinerants, women ready to go wherever the Gospel took them to evangelize and serve the poor. (Hugolino would win this part of the skirmish. Culture and the times could not conceive of women "on the streets" and without protection. Clare would eventually accept her cloistered status). However, even there, she would fashion her community unlike any other that existed at the time. The sisters would live in "mutual charity," making decisions in common, under the guidance of another sister who, though called abbess, would never act like an abbess of old. She would "wash the feet" of her sisters, rather than rule over them.

For the twenty-seven years that she outlived Francis, she never outgrew his memory or gave up on the fight to be an austere and poor community like the one Francis first created when he founded the Franciscan movement. She saw herself and her sisters as equal members of the First Order and of the original Franciscan movement. At the end of her life, she went on a hunger strike in order to protect her absolute poverty but also to secure the access her sisters had to the brothers of the First Order.

Canon law was being interpreted in such a way that would have restricted access of Franciscan brothers to the Lesser Sisters. This was inconceivable to Clare. How could sisters live without their brothers; how could the brothers survive in fraternity without their sisters? One needs to remember that, by this time, Clare had lived decades within the spirituality of Francis' "cosmic order," a cosmology of a "universal fraternity" that included lesser sisters and brothers, brother sun and sister moon, and mother/sister earth. One could not conceive of a world where brother sun refused to acknowledge or work in harmony with sister moon. Neither could Clare make sense of a Franciscan movement where access between sisters and brothers was rejected, neglected or canonically discontinued. Her hunger strike was a forceful and highly feminine way that she could reclaim the Franciscan movement as a bisexual reality, a gendered equality between women and men.

One sees Clare's radical courage and cleverness in using her body as a tool for resistance. Like Francis who regularly used his body as an important signifier of powerful doctrinal claims (i.e. standing naked in the public square, in the snow and on his deathbed), so Clare used her own body to shame the Church into recognizing and respecting the radical nature of discipleship for women.

She knew that men saw women's bodies as sites of nurturing and caring. Women's breasts fed the children. Women's hands tended the sick and the needy. Women's bodies rocked children to sleep and held the bodies of those in grief or distress to demonstrate kindness, compassion, and mutual charity.

A woman's body "on strike," in deep fasting, in resistance and protest was unthinkable and especially hard on men to comprehend or accept. Men are accustomed to "feminine space" as nurturing and giving, consoling and compassionate. They are not used to women's bodies that withdraw or withhold nurturance. It makes them sad, angry, confused and paralyzed, so powerful are the contradictory signs being displayed.[5]

Clare knows this and plays it masterfully. She cannot protest in the streets. The men have cloistered her. She cannot preach from the pulpits. She is not ordained. She can, however, speak from her bed and her chapel with the strongest force she has, her feminine body. Clare has fought her whole life so that her body, as a disciple of the Lord, is seen in a light and with a meaning that she gives it. She reads it in light of the Gospel and with her eyes constantly and intently on the Lord. She is not reading her body in secular terms or outside the biblical frame in which she has been educated. She is reading her body eucharistically and so she fasts to make a point about communion with her brothers for the sake of the Lesser Sisters.[6]

She will refuse to eat until the Pope provides assurance that her sisters can live poverty as absolutely and as fully as the men do and that her sisters will have equal and unfettered access to the brothers, at her discretion and not by consent of some male cardinal protector.

Finally, Clare was granted "the privilege of poverty." She won the argument and saved her community only hours before she died.

Clare as Theologian of Freedom and Hope

Notwithstanding the difficulties and disappointments or perhaps through them, Clare becomes a theologian of freedom and hope. The way that Clare develops her incarnation of Gospel poverty and uses the language of "mutual charity" to ground her unexpected and unprecedented actuation of feminine monastic life and the governance thereof are the fruits of a deep meditation on the lowliness of a God made man, a Christ expressing himself and his passion in humility.

Clare had lived in the violence of a greedy and mercenary culture. She wanted off the social grid that demanded that women be forced into marriage and become pawns to the social and economic privileges of men in her feudal world. On the night she escaped from the Door of Death to begin her life as a penitent, Clare knew exactly what she was doing. She wanted to do penance and to create a new ethical space for women

---

[5] Rudolf Bell, *Holy Anorexia* (Chicago: University of Chicago Press, 1985).

[6] Noel Muscat OFM, "I will always Defend You: St. Clare of Assisi and the Eucharist," accessed at: http://i-tau.com/franstudies/articles/Clare_&_Eucharist.pdf

to live the mutual love Clare discovered in evangelical poverty and in the Eucharist.[7]

Sharing that research with undergraduates has led me to the conclusion that Clare should be honored as the proto-feminist of Western culture. It was her activities back in the first half of the 13th century that led the way for the strides that have been made in the 20th and 21st centuries for women's rights, for their dignity and equality.

My study leads me to think of her as a theologian of freedom and of hope. Let me speak of the seven freedoms I see in her life and work as the first Franciscan woman.

THE SEVEN FREEDOMS OF CLARE OF ASSISI

It is hard for our post-modern minds to imagine that a largely cloistered woman of the 13th century could be considered a prophet of freedom and hope. She lived a supposed "sheltered life." She never traveled. The orbit of her life was limited to the hospice in which she worked, the garden and fields in which she tilled and grew food, the chapel in which she worshiped, and the hills and forests in which she prayed. These limits do not seem the right framework for the development of a proto-feminist's character and disposition.

However, one must ask what Clare did with the limits she faced and the obstacles she endured. The great psychologist and logotherapist, Viktor Frankl, once remarked that we may not be responsible for the circumstances of our lives, but we are responsible for what we do with those circumstances.

Many people and indeed perhaps most of us are bound by limits we wish we did not have. We are encumbered by circumstances that cramp the opportunities we wish we could take advantage of. Somehow, the truly wise and courageous among us, often in unseen ways and out of the blare of the media, do make a difference and accomplish amazing things for others. There are ordinary heroes among us who feed the sick, shelter the homeless, encourage the downcast, and provide motivation and inspiration to others that they can succeed. Every so often the media finds these "good news" stories that remind us that we were made for freedom and there are many times when those flowers must crack through rocks to fulfill our deep-down and grace-filled passion for life.

---

[7] Catherine M. Mooney, *Clare of Assisi and the Thirteenth-Century Church: Religious Women, Rules and Resistance* (Philadelphia: University of Pennsylvania Press, 2016).

Clare developed seven freedoms for herself and her sisters. A short meditation on each is in order.

1. Freedom to find God in her voice and through her experience

Clare grew up as a noblewoman in a rich and influential family whose castle overlooked the square in front of the cathedral of San Rufino. Her life was scripted by the conventions, customs and rituals that shaped cultural life in the 12th and 13th centuries. She learned the domestic arts and participated in them according to the level of her nobility (the servants did the hard work and drudgeries of daily life). She was educated not for debate and mutual conversations but with the goal of securing a strong and secure husband. She was her father's property and he would determine who she would marry. Her adolescence had an obvious trajectory toward an arranged marriage and the repetition of the domestic arts she had learned in her family with the children and the heirs she was expected to bear. The God to whom she would have learned to pray was a God who blessed these cultural and religious requirements.

Clare, for her part, saw something else and hoped for something more for her life. She couldn't be squeezed into the domestic constraints of noble life. She rejected an arranged marriage. She was an amazingly prayerful woman, even as an adolescent. Her concerns went beyond the simple aspirations of an adolescent girl. Her thoughts revolved around the poor and their needs. She spent her "free time" taking care of them.

Clare's first freedom is to find God in her own voice and through her experiences and not simply to mimic the customs and conventions of her time. By the time she was eighteen, she had already reflected enough on her own experience of God to realize that she must make a break and a decisive one, at that.

Her experience of God does not allow half-hearted measures or simplistic maneuvers that would only accommodate some spiritual nod toward the divine. Her experience of God is radical and deep and it demands everything from her. She willingly gives it.

Palm Sunday night demonstrates this. She is the master of its intrigue; she is the scriptwriter of its ingenuity. She knows the inner workings of the castle in which she lives; she knows the creaking sounds of its movements. From her castle window, she also knows her surroundings, peoples' usual comings and goings.

She knows when and how she is to move. Amazingly, she knows that she is going to dispose of all her belongings, all her holdings and all her inheritance *before* she arrives for tonsure at the hands of Francis. She manufactures this radical maneuver, because it is *her* decision and no one else's to follow Francis completely, without hesitation and with no turning back. She knows what she wants and she is going to achieve it, for the love of God.

2. *Freedom to live an intentional life of compassion and feminine "mutual charity"*

We have hinted above that what Clare is pursuing above all is an *intentional life*. She is seeking to live a life of her own making, following pursuits of her own persuasions. She has lived all her life by the dictates of culture and convention. She has done what was required of her as a good Christian noble woman of faith. She wants more, not against the Church but deep within it. She does not intend to walk away from the faith in order to pursue her dreams. Her dreams lie deeply within the Church. They are so deep that not even the men and women of her time recognize their source. It will take time for the people and priests of her age to understand or appreciate how Clare's intentions make up a radical new spiritual charism in the Church; they speak and have deep resonance with the mystical traditions found in Eucharistic theology. Clare has insights into communion from a young age that will only bear fruit in generations to come.

Thus, Clare seeks to live an intentional life of compassion and a feminine form of mutual charity. As we have noted above, the forms of religious life current in her time were designed for hierarchy, the separation of powers, for control of the passions and the smooth conduct of the habits of religious living. Effective religious were taught to live by the law and order of religious decorum and to find God's will precisely and unequivocally in obedience to the commands of a religious superior.

Clare finds something else. She is abbess in title only; she runs her convent as a lesser sister who wishes to serve her sisters in humility and generosity. She builds that form of leadership and governance in deep meditation on the Incarnation of Christ and his service of "mutual charity."

3. *FREEDOM TO LIVE A LIFE OF SIMPLICITY, OUTSIDE THE CUSTOMS AND NORMS EXPECTED OF WOMEN*

What Clare was looking for when she went through the "Door of Death" into that moonlit Palm Sunday night was the exhilarating fresh air of freedom. What enticed Clare into that break was what she saw in Francis' life and in the life of his brothers, as she watched them in the square and as she traveled to and from the churches of Assisi. She saw their simple freedom, the freedom to live in poverty, demanding nothing of anyone, depriving no one of anything. These were men who were generous because they had stopped requiring anything of others except kindness. They refused to fight for anything, because they were satisfied with whatever they had and hopeful for whatever might come from a good and provident God.

Clare knew the expectations placed on her from a very young age: an arranged marriage, a brood of healthy children, domestic chores, pleasant conversations, attendance at church, genial relations with servants, a protected life, an observed existence controlled by powerful men who promised (but sometimes didn't deliver on) the protections that women required.

Clare, on the other hand, wanted the air to breathe, the sun to warm her, the fields to feed her, and brothers and sisters who could converse with her about things that mattered to her: life and death, heaven and hell, saints and sinners, joys and anxieties, the Incarnate Christ and the Eucharist.

4. *FREEDOM TO LIVE AND EXPRESS A DIRECT FEMININE EXPERIENCE OF THE DIVINE, USING FEMININE EXPRESSIONS, SIGNS AND RITUALS*

It amazes us how long it took for Clare to be listened to by those assigned to protect her and her community. The bishops and cardinal and even some of the lesser brothers found it next to impossible to understand the signs and rituals that Clare was trying to shape from within her feminine understanding of Franciscan discipleship. Clare's governance of her community was decidedly feminine. The imagery she used for her own mystical experiences, besides being deeply Eucharistic, emerged from feminine intuitions about intimacy, closeness, engagement, conversation, and caring. Long before the works of Carol Gilligan and Mary Field Belenky find their arrival in our consciousness, there are women like Clare already positing spiritual images that cross and bend gender enough to break open new insights about the Incarnation, Passion, Death and Resurrection of the Lord. [8]

In her monastery of San Damiano, Clare constructs a world where women can imagine God from within their own feminine experiences and can test these out because Clare has created a new ethical space where women can practice the arts of feminine discourse, dialogue, compassionate and attentive listening, reconciliation and abiding patience through difficult times.

5. *Freedom to live a spirituality of feminine strength that challenges cultural conventions of women as "the weaker sex"*

Among her most amazing but often overlooked positive characteristics is Clare's spirituality of feminine strength. Clare proved herself a formidable adversary to popes and cardinals who underplayed or tried to undercut her commitment to full Franciscan discipleship. She refused to be protected from Francis' absolute poverty. She refused any sort of exception or exemption, simply because she was a woman. She wanted and intended to follow Christ, not half-heartedly or half way. She saw nothing in the Gospel that shrunk the discipleship of women and she was not going to let ecclesiastical customs or social conventions get in the way of her resolution to prove that women were just as strong as men (if not stronger) and women could follow Christ as fully and as personally as men.

Clare challenged the overwhelming cultural convention that women were the "weaker sex" in the Church. Her fasting and her disciplines were just as strong and of even longer duration than most of the men's. She knew the Incarnate Christ; she reverenced his Gospel and his commands; she celebrated his humility, especially in the Eucharist. She made the Eucharist the centerpiece of her approach to feminine governance. She knew that Christ in the Eucharist was humble. She also knew that, under that form of bread and wine, Christ was strong. Clare's humility should never be confused with weakness.

Francis had taught the brothers that Franciscan strength was to be found in minority, in taking the last place and in serving the needs of

[8] Carol Gilligan, *In A Different Voice: Psychological Theory and Women's Development* (Cambridge MA: Harvard University Press, 1984); M.F. Belenky, B.M. Clinchy, N.R. Goldberger and J.M. Tarule. 1986. *Women's Ways of Knowing: The Development of Self, Voice, and Mind* (New York: Basic Books, 1986); Catherine M. Mooney, *Gendered Voices: Medieval Saints and their Interpreters* (Philadelphia: University of Pennsylvania Press, 1999).

those who were vulnerable and on the margins of society. Francis found his strength in the paradoxes of perfect joy, as he reminds us in the story of how he might come to a friary late on a cold winter's night and be refused entrance. Even after announcing himself as Francis, the founder and minister of the Order, he would be told not to disturb the community, to go away and not come back.

Francis found his strength in the absolute minority of forgiveness and in accepting the event as humbly and generously as he could in imitation of the rejection that Jesus felt out of love on the Cross.

Clare wanted that sort of strength, that kind of humility, and she practiced it in the chapters and discussions with her sisters.

6. Freedom to have economic independence and construct relationships of collaboration and generosity.

Of all the dimensions of the Franciscan movement that women and men misunderstand the most, it is the reasons and motives for Franciscan poverty. Too many people outside the Orders and some within think that the reason for poverty is penitential and ascetical. That view holds that we vow poverty to castigate the world in some way, declaring it evil, wicked and sinful, largely because of its material temptations. It holds that the world is largely, if not wholly wicked or unhealthy, because it traps us in material goods and sensual desires. There is a deep tradition of that sort of thinking in Jewish and Christian thought. We find its roots in Gnosticism, Manicheanism, Stoicism, Puritanism, and all their modern derivatives.

Franciscanism understands poverty differently. The Lesser Brothers and Sisters (members of the three Franciscan Orders today, Third Order Regular Franciscans, and all Franciscan-hearted people) understand that the real purpose of poverty is relational, not ascetical. We hold on to poverty because it is the surest guarantee of our relationship with one another. Spirituality teaches us that stuff/things trap us in competitive relationships. We use things to dominate and deprive one another. Once when St. Francis was told by a bishop that he couldn't possibly live without "owning" things, Francis replied directly to him. He told the bishop that if he had things, he would need to protect them with violence. He chose not to own, so as not to become involved in violence and greed again.

We know how deeply violence and greed disturbed and distorted his adolescence. We know how Francis' dreams of knightly glory were fed by the dark desires for money and wealth. Francis found that, if he gave up the need to have, to control, to dominate and to deprive, he could live simply and joyfully. He could experience and share "pace e bene" (peace and all good). He could find a happiness that was durable and, indeed, eternal.

This is what Clare learned from her window overlooking the cathedral square. She wanted a world of sisterly and brotherly relationships. She had learned that lesson long before she met Francis. She was already recognized as a holy young woman long before she ever met Francis. She already had a deep devotion to the Blessed Sacrament and the humility of Christ found therein. As a young girl, she had developed a strong incarnational spirituality that joined all humanity and, indeed, all creation into a deep communion with God revealed as Father, Son, and Spirit.

The economic dependence foisted upon her by the customs and conventions of Assisi blocked her solidarity with the poor. She wanted to do more than offer them charity from the coffers of her rich father and uncles. She wanted to love the poor. She wanted to be compassion and mercy for them. She wanted to be the incarnate iteration of Christ's kindness in the Assisi of her time. She would never be able to do that in the protected and arranged world that she was handed. And so, she broke free and began to create an economic independence that would allow her to express her feminine love, compassion and generosity with her unique tenderness.

7. Freedom to develop a spirituality of the feminine body that upends the masculine definition of women's body as "evil" and "tempting." Focuses on women's bodies as "holy places" and not simply the site for men's desires.

We know the ancient and modern versions by which the feminine body is defined solely in terms of evil.[9] Christian literature is surfeited with doctrines and documents that recount the power of the woman's body to tempt men and lead the world into sin. We know how easily women's bodies are "objectified" and reduced simply to being "playthings" and objects of men's desire, always under the voyeuristic glance and authoritarian control of men who are doing the viewing. One of the great

[9] Suman Chakraborty, "Women, Serpent and Devil: Female Devilry in Hindu and Biblical Myth and its Cultural Representation: A Comparative Study". *Journal of International Women's Studies*, January 2017, 18(2), 156-165. Available at: http://vc.bridgew.edu/jiws/vol18/iss2/11.

advances of feminism is not to have women's bodies defined by men's desires. One of the great leaps forward of the so-called first and second waves of feminism in the 20th century was the description of the social geography of feminine life, so that feminine bodies were no longer to be seen as men's territory, wholly controlled by them, but were to be seen as a woman's "site," defined for feminine meaning and ultimate purpose.[10]

One might argue that one of the advances that Clare's embodied mysticism suggests is that women are brought out from under the imagery of their bodies as "evil" and "tempting." Instead, we learn that women's bodies are "holy places" capable of divine embraces, caresses, holy sensations that unite women to Christ and to the world.[11]

Clare's strong identification with the humble Christ and her spirituality of the "imitation of Christ" gives her immense confidence to look intently at her world in all of its simple elegance, lush diversity and holy authenticity.[12] She has worked with her hands; she has plowed the fields and harvested the crops along with her sisters. She knows her moral, spiritual and physical strength. She does not need to hide or mask her distinct feminine sensations. She writes:

> When you have loved [Him], You shall become chaste; when You have touched [Him], You shall become pure; when You have accepted [Him], you shall be a virgin ... Whose power is stronger... Whose appearance more beautiful... In Whose embrace you are already caught up. Who has adorned Your breast with precious stones and has placed priceless pearls in Your ears and has surrounded You with sparkling gems as though blossoms of springtime and placed on Your head a golden crown as a sign [to all] of Your holiness.[13]

It is true, Clare's words are "explicit and strong in their immediacy: caresses, possession, sexual union, virginity, and also the physical and material beauty of the body and its ornaments."[14]

---

[10] The Boston Women's Health Book Collaborative, *Our Bodies, Ourselves* revised (New York: Simon and Schuster, 2011).

[11] Elizabeth A. Esposito. *Embodying Mysticism: The Utilization of Embodied Experience in the Mysticism of Italian Women, Circa 1200-1400 CE* (MA Thesis, University of Florida, 2004).

[12] Catherine M. Mooney, "Imitatio Christi or Imitatio Mariae? Clare of Assisi and her Interpreters" in Catherine M. Mooney, ed. *Gendered Voices: Medieval Saints and Their Interpreters* (Philadelphia: University of Pennsylvania Press, 1999), 52-77.

[13] Clare's First Letter to Agnes.

[14] Mariateresa Fumagalli Beonio-Brocchieri, "The Feminine Mind in Medieval Mysticism," in *Creative Women in Medieval and Early Modem Italy: A Religious and Artistic*

What differentiates Clare's insights from much of today's feminist descriptions is that Clare sees women's bodies as both sensual and holy sites. Clare refuses to allow her body to become a slate on which any man (or woman), company or corporation can write whatever they wish and define however much they want the limits and parameters of her deepest and most transcendent desires. Clare challenges the 21st century's reconstructions of gender by claiming the feminine body as simultaneously sensual and sacramental.

CONCLUSION

Like Francis, Clare heard the cry of the victims of Assisi. She attended to the needs of the sick in the hospice of San Damiano. She gathered women around her who themselves were the victims of the cultural abuses, stereotypes and biases of their time. Unfortunately, the distance of time and the cultural conventions of their day don't allow us to peer more deeply into the shadows of those cultural conventions. However, we can surmise!

If greed and violence were the social constructs that impelled Francis and the lesser brothers to want off the social grid of pride and glory that captivated masculinity in Francis' day and age, what must have compelled women to make the even more dangerous and culturally unacceptable leap into the unknown of Franciscanism, as Clare and her sisters did? We know some of it. Economic independence, spiritual autonomy, gender strength and feminine integrity are the new social constructs that Clare and her sisters are embodying and developing for the women of their age.

Once again, we learn that Franciscanism is not based on text (although we have many good ones). It is a movement of rituals and gestures: Francis naked in the public square, in the snow and at the end of his life. Francis meeting the Sultan inside the Muslim camp at Damietta, Egypt. Clare in her midnight run to be tonsured by Francis and her sister, Agnes, doing the same sixteen days later, amid the deadly fury of her uncles and courtiers.

We know the heroism of their journeys not by what they wrote but largely by what they did. Fortunately, we have enough of what they wrote to catch the meaning of what they were enacting. Their rituals and gestures, however, speak to the drama of their passion and their convictions.

Renaissance (Philadelphia: University of Pennsylvania Press, 1994), 22.

Clare's medieval mind emerges as courageous, strong, forceful, empathic, consoling, compassionate and wonderfully feminine in imitation of the humble Christ and his simple disciple, Francis.

Questions for Reflection

1. In what ways can Clare of Assisi be seen as a role model for women suffering today from discrimination, harassment and injustice?

2. How does Clare's embodied mysticism illuminate a distinctive Franciscan theology of the body?

3. Clare developed a practice of feminine leadership as mutual charity. How does this challenge your community's leadership style?

4. What does it mean to read one's body eucharistically?

John's Story

From all appearances, John was one of the most gregarious, funny and engaging seminarians I had ever met. He was dedicated to prayer, compassionate with everyone he met, pastorally attuned to the needs of people, with not a hint of incipient clericalism. He never seemed to be trying to escape from some responsibility or procure some kind of privilege because he was going to be a priest. He seemed the kind of seminarian who genuinely and simply wanted to serve.

John was an excellent student. He understood the work of theology and never had to hide behind a rigid dogmatism or a timid relativism, a tendency of some seminarians who simply use theology for their authority needs. John was prudent enough to know where mystery started and ended. He had a genuine reverence for God and seemed to work hard at being humble in a mature adult way.

I was happy when John came to see me. I have learned over the years that, even the best and brightest of our students, whether in religion or out of it, live very complex and complicated lives. Sometimes the ones who appear to have it all must do a lot of praying, sacrificing, and suffering to make continuous progress before the Lord. John was one of them.

John was direct as he began to tell me what was on his mind. He had gotten "involved" with another seminarian. He knew it was wrong but he wanted to understand what it all meant. He ended the relationship before it progressed too far and in unhealthy ways, but he wanted to understand how he had gotten himself in such a sexually-provocative predicament, despite his best intentions and commitment to live a celibate life.

We spent weeks speaking about his life, his childhood and adolescence, what he had learned about intimacy and what frightened him about commitment. We looked for the various "triggers" to his anxiety, what set them off and how he handled them. There was enough stress in his life to recommend that he learn early what he could do and what he couldn't, what he should involve himself in and what he should allow others to do. The closer we got to his defenses, the more uncertain he became and the more real was the cloud that came over him.

One day he revealed what was really bothering him. He was sexually and provocatively approached years before by his parish priest in a van on their way to a beach get away. He admired this priest and looked up to him in many ways. The priest was known as a compassionate preacher, a man who was both down-to-earth and yet inspiring enough in his preaching to make the Gospel come alive. The assault was aggressive and emotionally painful. It happened and was never spoken about again, until the moment John shared it with me.

It was clear that there was a split between John's outer voice and inner voice. His outer voice, the one which he shared with others, was filled with laughter and joy, with optimism and resonances of hope. His inner voice, the one with which he spoke to himself and to God, was tormented. In many ways, he blamed himself for the assault. He should have seen it coming; he should have seen the warning signs; he should have stopped it the moment "things went too far." He should have spoken about his confusing feelings to the priest, gotten angry and, as he said, "decked him out." Instead, he froze.

His inner voice was quite frozen, paralyzed in feelings he barely understood and could hardly articulate. Over the many months that we spoke, his inner voice changed in timber and strength. Being in a safe space, without judgment, allowed him to explore all sides of his emotional world. He could trust his sunny and optimistic side and he could allow his angry and explosive side to find a genuine outlet.

He began to understand that his "involvement" with another seminarian was not a sign of his depravity, as his inner voice demanded him to think, but a "cry for help." The awful secret, the torment within, the violent assault he had experienced at the hands of a man he admired, all of this had to come forward and did so in the awkward way that the psyche often uses to get our attention.

Our conversations were, in my view, only partially successful. I encouraged John to take other steps: to confront the man who assaulted him and publicly name him. John was not ready to do this. He was satisfied with the emotional progress he had made, grateful for the self-knowledge he had gained and the mature boundaries he had established to protect himself from unwanted sexual advances and exploitations.

I ended my pastoral counseling practice not long after. I saw a greater challenge on the horizon and that was the "conversion" of systems and structures in the church. So much of my psychological training had been on helping individual priests and religious get healthier. My studies at the Institute of Psychology in Rome had been based on solid scientific research on the specific psychodynamics of those in religion. We had amassed an impressive array of data on the conflicts and inconsistencies that religious women and men face as they attempt to live out their vocational calls. That theory of self-transcendent consistency translated into powerful psychotherapeutic techniques for my colleagues in the burgeoning field.[1]

Another insight had emerged in my research of the psychological dynamics of religious women and men and it had to do with the social-psychological systems in which they were inserted, inextricably linked and sometimes enmeshed. It was my respectful conclusion that, despite his genius as a psychiatrist and clinical psychologist, Luigi Rulla SJ (under whom I had studied at the Institute of Psychology in Rome) had not gone far enough in his analysis. He failed to take notice of the ways that systems maintain us in our unhealthy patterns of belief and action. Further training at the Ackerman Institute for Family Therapy in New York and the Organizational Development Program at the William Alanson White Institute for Psychiatry added new layers of insight to my own theoretical hold and psychological practice when dealing with victims. Here is how I expressed the challenge I faced.

> By way of critique of Rulla's contribution, we can offer the following. Rulla's theory of self-transcendent consistency and the research that supports it are an elaborate and intricate analysis of the intrapsychic dynamics that attend the construction, maintenance and development of self-transcendent values in vocational life. Rulla's attention is drawn to two areas of conversion in religious life, the personal and the interpersonal. The methods of formation he provides for growth in vocational life are those which attend these two areas of conversion. Vocational growth sessions, along with proportionate and supported pastoral experiences, have been shown to be powerful and, indeed, essential mechanisms for increasing the capacity to internalize the self-transcendent values of religion.[2]
>
> But, they are insufficient. Rulla leaves largely unexamined the social and organizational dynamics of contemporary institutions. What is missing from Rulla's theory and the research of

[1] Luigi M. Rulla, *Psychological Structure and Vocation*, 3rd edition (Rome: Gregorian University Press, 1995); Luigi M. Rulla, Joyce Ridick and Franco Imoda, *Anthropology of the Christian Vocation: Existential Confirmation, Vol. II.* (Rome: Gregorian University Press, 1989).

[2] Rulla, Ridick and Imoda, *ACVII*, 177-225.

Rulla, Ridick and Imoda is a concentration on the "workplace within" and the "psychodynamics of organizational life."[3]

Rulla himself admits that his theory is best applied to internal rather than external structures, when he writes:

The anthropology here proposed as a Christian personalism concentrates on structures inside the person rather than on structures outside the person; that is, on structures which help one become what one is: a being which is by nature called to theocentric self-transcendence so as to be able to love the Divine You and the human you in a responsible way, with the help of grace. Moreover, this anthropology takes account of the existential situation of the person as a being who must overcome conscious and subconscious limitations on freedom (limitations which, nevertheless, do not diminish the person's basic responsibility). The helps to formation suggested in this tenth section, both for the intrapersonal and interpersonal areas, are meant as a modest contribution to assist the human person in his dialogue with the indispensable and primary communication of God's grace.[4]

Rulla offers the rationale for why he limited himself to the intrapersonal and interpersonal dimensions of religious life. He writes tellingly:

It is the divisions, inconsistencies, and disharmonies, conscious and unconscious, lying within the individual human heart, which provoke and sustain the external injustices, disunities, and fractures of society.[5]

Left largely untreated in Rulla's work is how these personal divisions are transformed into structural inconsistencies and, indeed, how they become social or structural sin "embedded or expressed in the institutions, structures, and conventions of social, political, economic and cultural life."[6]

---

[3] Larry Hirschhorn, *The Workplace Within: Psychodynamics of Organizational Life* (Cambridge, MA: MIT Press, 1993).

[4] Rulla, *ACVI,* 452.

[5] *Ibid.,* 455.

[6] Bryan N. Massingale, *The Social Dimensions of Sin and Reconciliation in the Theologies of James H. Cone and Gustavo Gutierrez* (Rome: Pontificia Universitas Alphonsianum, 1991), 333.

> It is as if Rulla is unaware of how *structures of sin* are created and maintained not only by individuals but also by groups. Massingale, however, demonstrates how social or structural sins arise in a group or culture, how they affect us and how they double back as (reinforcing) inducements to personal (and social) sin.[7] In fact, injustice often hides in the conventions, customs, and systems of organizations, including religious ones. Having morphed into structures of sin or, as we shall see in the next chapter, "social defenses," the conventions appear normal and "just the way things are," when, in fact, they carry group biases and cultural discrimination.
>
> Today, religious communities face a world of increasing diversity and an ever more dangerous disparity.[8] It seems clear that *international* issues will take up more and more of our moral imagination as religious leaders in the 21st century. Religious communities are undergoing a profound process of organizational challenge and transformation. A chronic vocational shortage now threatens the institutional viability and structural integrity of many religious congregations in the United States.[9]
>
> Given the power of organizational forces both within and without religious congregations, it appears that the tools and methods of an intrapersonal and interpersonal psychological approach are a necessary but insufficient foundation for an understanding of the fraternal economy.[10]

John's situation and Rulla's research lead to a fundamental new dimension of what it means to "listen to the cry of the victims." It is not enough to remain with individual empathy or personal sympathy. These are critically important but insufficient. When it comes to the victimization of the poor and vulnerable, we are dealing with more than personal bias and individual discrimination. We are dealing with power dynamics and structural inequalities. Injustice is carried out by

---

[7] *Ibid.*, 330.

[8] David B. Couturier, "From Diversity to Disparity: The Structural Conversion of Religious Life," *Horizon* 14:4 (Fall, 1989), 23-28.

[9] D.J. Nygren and M.D. Ukeritis, *The Future of Religious Orders in the United States* (Westport, CT: Praeger, 1993).

[10] David B. Couturier, *Franciscans and their Finances: Economics in a Disenchanted World* (St. Bonaventure, NY: Franciscan Institute Publications, 2015), 167-169.

individuals who are often protected, shielded, and sheltered by systems that are already imposing to those made vulnerable by their suffering.

There was another step that needed to be taken in John's case. It was not enough to relieve John's presenting problem, although it is always the choice of mature adults when to start and when to conclude their counseling or spiritual direction. It may have been of further help to be a part of an effort that would dismantle the system that shielded and sheltered the man who assaulted him.

Therefore, my efforts as a scholar and researcher turned toward "structural conversion," developing the tools, skills and theory needed by which pastoral systems could diagnose their corporate health and remove the social defenses and institutional mechanisms by which inappropriate behaviors are tolerated and advanced in the very systems meant to bring pastoral care and comfort.

It was John's case, among others, that convinced me to begin a new practice and a new dimension of how to hear the voice of victims and the voice of the crucified in the world today.

Question for Reflection

1. Listening to the cry of victims requires systemic and structural change. What new institutional practices are needed to sustain a commitment to the victims of injustice in your local church or community?

Chapter Six

Reversing the Negative

The premise of this book has been that the path to the renewal of Church life in general and Franciscan life in particular is by way of the "vox victimarum," a new and attentive listening to the victims of history, a turning away from the patterns of forgetfulness and amnesia that characterize modernity's belief in inevitable human progress. It requires of us a deep recovery of our primal and original memories of the faith through an attentive listening that leads to action on behalf of those who suffer the most on the margins of society.

We spoke first of the attentive listening we must accord to the Jewish slaves in the brickyards of Egypt, for it was there, in the most unlikely place of history, that Yahweh heard the cries of the poor and acted. In this, we must forego our Enlightenment prejudice that religion is not political and that it is not interested in matters of state. That prejudice was the construction of philosophers from Machiavelli to Hobbes, from Kant to Harris, who wish to supplant doctrine with secular reason. To do so, they must ignore the Scriptural evidence and its mandate that God became political when God commanded Moses to go to Pharaoh in order that Pharaoh release his labor force for the sake of covenant and justice.

We spoke of Jesus' prophetic ministry as the fulfillment of the power of the "vox victimarum." The God who once heard the cry of Abel in his death throes at the hands of his brother, Cain, now hears the cry of Jesus on the Cross. Jesus, as James Alison asserts, is the true Victim of the Roman Empire's reign of brutality. He is the Victim who gathers with him at the Cross all those who have been murdered, lied to, betrayed, cheated, robbed of their possessions or good name, those who have suffered from humanity's betrayal of its call to be "the beloved" of God. Jesus brings with Him to the Cross the tax collectors and the prostitutes, Lazarus at the gate and the Jew in the ditch. He makes their cry His own, as He surrenders all that He is and all the lost sheep He has gathered to the ultimate mercy and compassion of Yahweh.

Francis and Clare, each in their own distinct way, recover their memory of the poor as the path to their much-needed redemption from the greed and violence of their day. We know that Francis spent his adolescence in a failed plan to achieve glory and with a deep repugnance for lepers and anyone who was sick and vulnerable. Thomas of Celano, Francis' biographer, reminds us that he would pinch his nose in deep disgust whenever he came within two miles of a leper hospice outside the city limits of Assisi. He began to recover his mind and his soul when he learned to embrace and serve the lepers.

Francis went from disgust to dignity because his attentive listening changed the framework of how he thought and acted, in a way that released him for life and love. I think the encounter and embrace of the leper indicates more than what we have traditionally understood. In our usual telling, Francis is the hero of that encounter. He embraces the leper, despite his disgust. In our ordinary telling, the leper is simply the passive recipient of the encounter, the mute receptacle of the incipient saint's generous compassion.

I think we have to "reverse the negative" here.[1] What if the leper is not the passive partner in this scene, but the more active agent of compassion and kindness? If we reverse the negative, we see the outlines of a new dynamic. We see the more compelling act of compassion and generosity on the part of the leper.

The leper's wounds are skin-deep. Francis' history of disgust and dismissal of the leper are soul-deep. They go beyond tissue and bone; they corrupt Francis' soul and atrophy his heart. When the leper embraces Francis, he recognizes and accords a new dignity to Francis. He allows Francis communion with him. He recognizes Francis' disgust; it was probably well-known to the lepers in the small town that was Assisi at the time. The leper probably knew the history of revulsion and rejection that the adolescent Francis had for him. And yet, the leper hears the cry of the poor Francis. The leper does mercy on Francis. The leper is more than a passive recipient of mercy; the leper is an active partner in the recovery of Francis' spirit by embracing Francis, not returning disgust with disgust. The leper knows Francis' wound but sees Francis' dignity. Francis remains touched and grateful to the leper for having loved him in his disgust, when Francis' faults were more than skin-deep. It was the arrogant Francis that the leper embraced and changed.

---

[1] I thank Joseph Chinnici for this intriguing image and insight. The initial image is wonderfully his. I am taking it in a new direction.

I want to spend a few moments now suggesting how "reversing the negative" to hear the voice of victims and the forgotten is the way that we must proceed if we are to renew Franciscan life in the 21st century.

By "reversing the negative," I mean, along with Chinicci, the technique that was used to see the outline of the dead Christ in the Shroud of Turin. To the naked eye, the Shroud looks like a long piece of cloth with what look like random splatters of blood and dirt all over it. However, when we look more closely, when we photograph the shroud and look at the negative of it, we see the stark outline of a crucified man, with nail marks in his hands and side.

We need to "reverse the negative" and take another look at our history beyond the ordinary and obvious ways that we are used to. We are learning the hard way that the ordinary ways that we have been looking at the church and society today are dysfunctional and self-serving. Our ordinary methods of church discernment are deeply flawed, in part because they have been and they remain protective of clerical privileges at the expense of the suffering of those we are supposed to love and serve.

We will not recover from our scandals by our ordinary means of analysis and discernment, because we cannot see, we cannot feel, and we cannot experience the depths of horror experienced by the poor and by abused children by our ordinary inherited means. That is clear. We have decades' worth of experience across the globe, at every level of the church, that now verify how blind we have been, how deaf we have become to the first act of covenant and of the beloved community, to hear the cry of the poor.

I have asked the question in about as stark and as painful a way as I could muster (and it hurts to say it this way). "How did the church, meant to be the 'beloved community of the Lord,' become a culture of cruelty and corruption? How did this happen? What must we do about it? Remember the words of Cardinal Sean O'Malley on the stakes we face, "Catholics have lost patience with us and civil society has lost confidence in us."

How do we "reverse the negative" and see what is unseen by the naked eye and hear what cannot be heard by the naked ear?

Reversing the Negative as a Spiritual Dynamic

By "reversing the negative," I mean a spiritual practice of looking for what has been overlooked, making visible what has been hidden, listening for what has been muffled or muted and making what has been behind the scenes and below consciousness foremost in our attention and awareness.

As we have seen in the life and work of Francis of Assisi, he did not invent the humility of God. It was always within the doctrine of the Church and the spirituality of the people of God. However, it had been suppressed and overtaken by meditations, practices and rituals that emphasized the majesty of God, the glory of the divine, and the omniscience of the Lord. Francis' project was to pose a question to himself, his sisters and brothers, and the whole church –"who am I, what is God and who are we as a people when seen from the position of the last place? Is God's graciousness as abundant and full at the end of the line as it is at the front of line?"

Francis did not invent "minority" as a virtue of the spiritual life; he simply raised it to consciousness and made it the primary and working dynamic of his Order. No founder had done that before. Previous founders made other virtues central: penance, solitude, work and prayer. None thought of making "minority" the central virtue around which all others orbited. Minority is a radical experiment of faith that challenges us still today. Minority means voluntarily ceding one's place at the top, in the front, above everyone else in all things and every circumstance so as to experience the tenderness and mercy of God, as revealed in the Beatitudes as belonging to the meek and humble of heart.

It is counter-cultural and counter-intuitive in a society immersed in a philosophy, as Walter Brueggemann describes it, of "self-invention for self-sufficiency." The philosophical systems we have inherited, the cultural patterns we have received, all point to a social and psychological mandate to compete aggressively against one another so as to be number one, subservient to nothing and no one except ourselves in our self-sufficiency. This is surely the economic philosophy that drives our consumerist culture with its principles of self-advancement and self-promotion, our creeds of personal ambition and individual entitlement.

Minority is our primary Franciscan act of cultural disruption in a society that disparages, demeans and dismisses those who are economically vulnerable and socially deprived on account of their perceived and projected inferiority because of race, class, gender or sexual orientation. Social customs and norms dictate prejudice toward those already privileged and bias against those simply struggling to survive through devastating illnesses or serious downturns in the economy.

Recently, I published an article with the very bulky title, "Migration, Childhood and Trump's Metaphors of Disenchantment: A Franciscan

Critical Discourse Analysis."[2] Trust me, I do not want to feed into the political polarization that drives so much of our media today. I am not promoting a pro-Trumpian or an anti-Trumpian political stance. My allegiance is to Franciscanism, not to the Democratic or Republican party. My article was an attempt to analyze the metaphors, images, word-pictures that President Trump has been using to describe the children of legal and illegal immigrants in order to understand how his administration is asking us to think about children, their development and their future.

My analysis is a socio-analytical one (and hopefully a spiritual exercise, as well). I begin with the work of psychologist Bruno Bettelheim on "the uses of enchantment" in childhood development.[3] Bettelheim studies fairy tales and fables, like Little Red Riding Hood and Jack and the Bean Stalk, in order to understand how children employ these fables to confront their fears and anxieties in front of larger, more imposing and "dangerous" adult figures, including their parents. These fairy tales and fables help children negotiate and resolve their conflicts with their parents and other adults by helping them understand the origin and course, the whys and wherefores of life in a world run by adults and not children. These fables tell children what we really think about them as they are growing up.

Remembering this line of research from my early studies in developmental psychology, I wondered what Trump's metaphors, his use of images regarding immigrant children, tell children (and us) what we think about them when they are in trouble or distress. I wanted to learn how his use of metaphors and images teach us how we are supposed to feel and react to children with black or brown faces, clearly the most socially and economically vulnerable part of our entire American population.

The ordinary way we are supposed to receive these Trump speeches, one supposes, is as "political theater," bombastic imagery meant to disrupt the paralysis and ineffectiveness of Washington. We are told they are designed 'explosively' to rally action that protects American citizens in furtherance of a greater and more prosperous economy for all. That is, after all, the stated Trump doctrine and agenda. That sort of agenda might appear laudable. Who is not for the end of an ineffective Congressional system? Who is not for a more prosperous America?

However, if we reverse the negative of these images, what do we see? We have been trained and we are expected in our hot and severely

---

[2] David B. Couturier, "Migration, Childhood and Trump's Metaphors of Disenchantment: A Franciscan Critical Discourse Analysis," *Franciscan Connections/The Cord* 68:2 (Summer 2018), 32-40.

[3] Bruno Bettelheim, *The Uses of Enchantment: The Meaning and Importance of Fairy Tales* (New York: Alfred A. Knopf, 1976), 47.

polarized post-modern discourse to understand these images as nothing more than theater, innocuous even if bombastic political rhetoric aimed at adults who are weak and ineffective in their duties to protect the nation and advance the cause of liberty. If we "reverse the negative," and look at and feel through these images from the perspective of the most vulnerable among us, minority children, we see horrifying images and dangerous descriptions of children.

The images that are revealed when we reverse the negative of Trump's metaphors reveal desperate fears and troubling anxieties about children.

The new images of immigration are disturbing metaphors of danger, disease and terror directed at and perpetrated by minority children. Children are not to be protected because they are vulnerable. They are to be expelled because they are diseased, disturbed and dangerous. These new metaphors contradict the transformative myths of inclusion, goodness and beauty that the Franciscan message is meant to convey.

Minority forces us as Franciscans from our usual and habitual cultural perches, the ones that are culturally convenient and socially normative. Minority forces us to discern images and actions not from the position of comfort or certified self-interests, as the world of self-sufficiency requires us to do, but from the position of those weakest among us, those most vulnerable and least able to protect themselves by ordinary and available political means.

Reversing the Negative: Laity

For the past five hundred years, since the time of the Counter-Reformation, we, as Catholics and as religious, have been obsessed with clerical Orders. It is understandable. The Catholic Church felt itself under attack from the Reformers, some of whom dismantled the sacramental system of the church and denied any mediating role or sacramental significance to priests and bishops. The Church knew it had a clerical crisis on its hands. Even its own cardinalatial commission had published a sordid and damning report on the state of clergy at the time of the Reformation. However, the Catholic Church became highly defensive. Its language became provocatively condemnatory. Popes produced untold number of anathemas against anyone who disagreed with the magisterium. The power of bishops and popes accelerated exponentially culminating in the dogma of papal infallibility in the nineteenth century. Even Vatican II, with what Rahner called its "anthropological turn toward the subject" had only one major doctrinal issue to decide and it had to do with episcopal power. It asked the question – do bishops derive their power directly from Christ, as the apostles did, or are they simply delegates of the pope? What is the true status of Holy Orders?

In the wake of the Reformation, the Church asked itself over the course of hundreds of years what kind of power does the Pope have and what kind of jurisdiction does he enjoy? One has only to look at the clips of the coronation of John XXIII in 1958 to see how deep papal power and prerogatives were. John XXIII was carried into St. Peter's Square with the rituals and vestures of an Emperor. His courtiers had feathered fans; his guards had unsheathed swords to salute him; the Pope was crowned not with a single but with a triple tiara; and his Cardinals not only kissed his ring but also his foot.

He was not the only evidence of an obsession with the prerogatives and privileges of Holy Orders, so were the cascading ranks of cardinals, bishops, and multi-levels of proto-notaries and monsignors, draped in thirty-foot trains of silk and ermine, scarlet and fuscia-colored cassocks, with 12-point miters and multi-colored birettas. The processions and the liturgies were highly choreographed and totally clerical. There were no laity involved and no women participating in the coronation. This was a demonstration of the fullness of clerical power in and over the Church.

There was always the one, somewhat amusing tradition in the liturgy that came and went without much fanfare. As you may know, in papal processions the Holy Father is always the last to enter, since he enjoys the highest rank in the Church. Capuchins go first in papal processions, because they are deemed those of the lowest rank in the Church. (For that reason, we always get the worst seats in the house.)

Traditionally Capuchins had one more function in papal coronations and it came after all the pomp and circumstance were over and the Pope sat gloriously enthroned, fully bejeweled and crowned as sovereign of the Church. It was then that a Capuchin in his simple brown robes approached the Pope with sheaves of straw in his trembling hands. He waved them in the face of the newly crowned Supreme Pontiff and proclaimed: "Sic transit gloria mundi." So goes the glory of the world – nothing but straw, soon to be ashes. Honestly, it's my favorite part of the old rituals. It is a form of comic disruption, as only a Capuchin can do, of all the ostentation and regalia of Holy Orders. Capuchins have a knack for "reversing the negative."

As Christians, we need to ask ourselves, as honestly as we can, how deep and how extensive in us are those hundreds of years of training, images, rituals and experiences of clericalism? How much did it affect us and how much does it still shape our attitudes and our perceptions?

I don't simply mean how it affected priests and bishops. How did it affect all of us and how did it shape the spiritual images and ecclesial expectations we have of ourselves, in whatever segment of the church to which we belong and out of which we minister, as religious men or women, lay women or lay men?

In my own experience, I know only a few friars who are brazenly clerical in their disposition and their posture in the Church. Only a few still expect notice, respect, deference, privileges, exemptions and unquestioned admiration and reverence simply because they are priests. (I see it among religious brothers and religious sisters, as well, but it is fairly rare.)

However, this is not the "reversing (of) the negative" that I am suggesting. Our clericalism today is not as brazen and outright as it used to be, when we lived by all sorts of cultural customs of unquestioning deference to police, politicians, judges, nuns and priests.

What I want to suggest is that we need to look for more subtle signs, more covert evidence of structured privation and privilege within the Church, the ones that are more difficult to notice, because they have become so "normalized."

In her new book published by Franciscan Institute Publications, *Enduring Presence: Diversity and Authenticity among the First Generations of Franciscan Laity,* Dr. Darleen Pryds makes the following startling claim:

> Despite their enduring presence, the lay people who have lived according to Franciscan values and tenets have largely been overlooked and ignored in both academic and church settings. There are many reasons for this. First and foremost, the majority of lay
>
> Franciscans through the centuries have rarely brought attention to themselves. They generally did not announce their presence through distinctive dress, although some of them wore a habit or were issued a habit symbolically. Nor did they necessarily make their spiritual quests known through publicly witnessed vows, opting instead to make private commitments. Many lay Franciscans never joined the Third Order (today known as the Secular Order) either because it did not yet exist or because it was not necessary for their vocational interests. In a larger community—especially an official order—their works of faith and personal beliefs would likely get documented at least in official sorts of ways. But when laity live out their vocations as "freelancers,"

> they are on their own, usually under the radar of historical investigation. Finally, in some cases there were administrative efforts to suppress records of laity in the Franciscan fold.[4]

Pryds' thesis is stark and provocative. She is telling us that we do not know the full story of our own Franciscanism. There is a history of which we are mostly ignorant and unaware. That is so because that history has been hijacked and suppressed in favor of clerical and religious life interests, a privilege that we fail to admit and acknowledge.

We think we know the story of the laity in the Franciscan movement because we have had experience and some knowledge of the Secular Franciscan Order. However, as Pryds lays out her case, we begin to realize "many lay Franciscans never joined the Third Order... either because it did not yet exist or because it was not necessary for their vocational interests." She reminds us that, because of their non-canonical status, these lay Franciscans have remained "under the radar of historical investigation" and have been prone to the suppression of their stories as laity in the Franciscan fold, until now.

We are coming to the end of our long clerical obsession. We are being forced there! The dream of Vatican II for a deeper appreciation of lay spirituality based on baptism never found solid and healthy ground in which to flourish, not always because of bad will and malevolent intentions. The case could be made that we didn't know what we didn't know. As Franciscans today, we have to admit that we do not know the stories of many Franciscan laity that shaped the Franciscan movement from its earliest days. We have been so concentrated on our own drama as religious, so mesmerized by the great Franciscan theologians like Bonaventure, Peter of John Olivi, Alexander of Hales, and John Duns Scotus that we have not yet heard the voices of Franciscan laity.

Darleen Pryds tells those stories and I will leave it to you to read them carefully, as she masterfully presents them. Let me simply give you some of her conclusions about the characteristics of lay Franciscans that her research brings to the fore:

[4] Darleen Pryds, *Enduring Presence: Diversity and Authenticity among the First Generations of Franciscan Laity* (St. Bonaventure, NY: Franciscan Institute Publications, 2018).

Characteristics of Lay Franciscans[5]

Dr. Pryds writes her conclusions about the characteristics of lay Franciscans in this way:

1. Lay Franciscans participate in the Franciscan intellectual tradition by how they live more than by what they write. Theirs is an embodied theology and an embodied spirituality. Theirs is not a theology that is debated or disputed in academic forums. It may be considered a theology and a spirituality that is preached, but it is necessary to keep in mind that preaching in the 13th century was a diverse activity that could include liturgical homiletics, but more often included public reflections and public spectacle. In other words, most preaching in 13th-century Europe was street preaching, and that was the kind of evangelization that some lay Franciscans—both men and women—took up. But far more common was the lay Franciscan who lived out their spiritual calling in humble and often overlooked ways.

2. Lay Franciscans modeled their lives on Francis rather than Clare. Most lay Franciscans would not have had direct contact with Clare and would not have heard much about Clare. Francis and his fellow friars were visible in the streets and influenced laity who chose to follow them in their spiritual way of life as much as they could.

3. Lay Franciscans usually expressed their religious devotion in physically expressive ways. Even those who may have lived their lives in enclosed cells often did so in highly public cells, attached to centrally located churches that functioned as important gathering places for local laity. Therefore, even if they were enclosed, lay Franciscans were known in their communities by how they lived out their vocations. I have called this form of piety "performative."

4. Many lay Franciscans, especially women, suffered detractors and were included in both public and private episodes of derision.

5. Lay Franciscans usually persevered in their faith, despite (or perhaps because) of receiving criticism from peers. Now that I am looking at a broader and more complex group of subjects, I can see that

[5] This section is taken directly from the work of Darleen Pryds, *Enduring Presence, op.cit.*

while these faithful laity usually persevere in their faith, they do not always remain Franciscan in their chosen spiritual affiliation. For social reasons and for reasons of practical support, some faithful laity jump camps, choosing to affiliate with other mendicant orders, especially the Dominicans. Margaret of Città di Castello, after her traumatic experiences with Franciscans, is thought to have become a lay Dominican. And in at least one case, it remains unclear if the pious layman, Peter Pettinaio (the Combmaker), actually jumped into the Dominican camp or if Dominicans and Franciscans subsequently both claimed Peter as one of their own.

6. Franciscan laity adapt their lives to meet new challenges and to respond to new spiritual identities. They were flexible in their vocations of work and often changed their work as a result of their spiritual conversions.

7. Franciscan laity, like vowed members of the First and Second Orders, drew their spiritual inspiration from their deep faith in Christ and often cultivated an empathic spirituality from identifying with the suffering of Christ. Prayer practices such as contemplation and gazing on images of the crucified Christ helped lay Franciscans cultivate this piety, which was not an end in and of itself. Instead, their reflection on the suffering of Christ allowed them to feel and express empathy and compassion for others suffering around them.

8. Hospitality is a quality that is traditionally associated with Benedictine spirituality, but there are elements of it in the Franciscan charism, as well. How members of the different branches of the Franciscan family practiced hospitality varied. The most obvious displays of it came from the Franciscan laity with their possessions, homes, and livelihoods, which many of them used as an integral part of their spiritual practice by offering lodging and material sustenance to those in need. Lay Franciscans—whether they took official vows with the Third Order or not—owned property in ways that members of the first two orders did not. They were generous in sharing what they owned with others, especially with Friars, the Poor Clare Sisters, and with several lesser known lay faithful whom we will encounter in the following pages. Hospitality, then, is very much part of the Franciscan tradition, but it was practiced most fully among lay Franciscans since they had property to share unlike the members of the First or Second Order."

Pryds' work, above (1-8), reminds us that we need to be introduced to the complexities, surprises, and new ways of thinking about being Franciscan that we have not yet experienced or imagined. This will challenge us with alternative ways of approaching the Gospel of Christ in an authentic but diverse manner.

Conclusions

If our study of the voices of victims reveals anything, it is that we cannot continue on the path we have been walking. The people of God have lost patience with us and civil society has lost confidence in us. Too many have already decided that the only thing they can morally, ethically and spiritually do in the light of our worldwide scandals is to walk away or let the church wither away and leave the world to its profoundly secular imagination.

Many of us have seen the crisis coming. We know what Matthew Arnold meant when he famously wrote his poem, Dover Beach, back in 1867:

The Sea of Faith
Was once, too, at the full, and round earth's shore
Lay like the folds of a bright girdle furled.
But now I only hear
Its melancholy, long, withdrawing roar,
Retreating, to the breath
Of the night-wind, down the vast edges drear
And naked shingles of the world.

Ah, love, let us be true
To one another! for the world, which seems
To lie before us like a land of dreams,
So various, so beautiful, so new,
Hath really neither joy, nor love, nor light,
Nor certitude, nor peace, nor help for pain;
And we are here as on a darkling plain
Swept with confused alarms of struggle and flight,
Where ignorant armies clash by night.

We knew what Arnold was posing to us. We understood the immense challenges religion was facing in the crosswinds of secularism and consumerism. We took our vows and we took our chances on faith, determined to meet the obligations of religion with as much courage as we could muster.

My own research on the psychological and organizational dynamics of religion also convince me that we also took sides. Peter Steinfels reminded us of this in his book about American Catholicism, *A People Adrift: The Crisis of the Catholic Church in America.*[6] In that book, he posited that the American Catholic church was hopelessly deadlocked between liberals and conservatives, between those who read the signs of the time in a progressive light and those who see the same only from a traditionalist perspective. We have lived our faith during these past few decades in a very anxious way, passing from the Cold War and into the age of terrorism. To manage that anxiety, we have locked ourselves into convenient streams of thought, split narratives that we honestly believed would meet people's needs for freedom and agency in a difficult world.

The question I want to leave us with as an ongoing project, because this is not something that is going to be solved easily or without a major transformation, is this: have we really heard the cry of the victims of history and have we really listened to the hopes and anxieties of the laity in our church? Or, have we been so intent on being certain and sure about dogma, correct about liturgy, and precise about our theological positions that we missed the first act of a faith-filled justice -- to hear the cry of the poor?

Yahweh first heard the cry in the brickyards of Egypt; Jesus then heard it on the treacherous streets of Jerusalem and Galilee; Francis heard it as well when he encountered the leper by the side of the road. And we are challenged to hear it, as we must, not through the filters of our previous privileges and exemptions, but in its most raw and primitive screams from the mouth of victims today. We must hear it first from the victims of sexual abuse but also from all those disadvantaged and dismissed by the power plays and economic games that privilege the rich and powerful of this world, in the Church and out of it.

There is a part of us that wishes to avoid this Gethsemane of solidarity. It is understandable given all that we have endured thus far. And yet, our faith tells us of the rewards that accrue, the dignity that is achieved, when the meek and the poor take charge of their lives in minority. They are blessed in heart and spirit.

---

[6] Peter Steinfels, *A People Adrift: The Crisis of the Roman Catholic Church in America* (New York: Simon and Schuster, 2004).

Questions for Reflection

1. "Reversing the negative" is a technique by which we uncover truths hidden from ordinary means of analysis and study. Name a situation in your life, ministry or work that looks differently when this technique is applied to it.

2. How has the Church's historic obsession with Holy Orders affected your view and experience of Church life? In what ways can you affirm and strengthen lay spirituality?

The Vox Victimarum: Concluding Thoughts

In my career and ministry in the practice of psychology and organizational development, my thoughts have often turned to the questions of justice, one in particular. Why do those who proclaim goodness and profess to want justice fail to do so regularly and consistently? What motivates those who are committed to charity and solidarity to turn away in pursuit of other needs or agenda? The first paper I ever published was on seminarians and their capacity to promote justice.[1] At the time, the American bishops had added "the capacity to promote justice" as a required skill for those pursuing priesthood according to the prescriptions contained in the "Program for Priestly Formation." It seemed clear that few knew that skill's requirements or meaning. The paper looked at the psychological challenges involved in motivating seminarians to a deeper solidarity with the victims of injustice.

This small book turns our attention to the cry of victims throughout our religious history and asks us to learn how to pay attention again, how to focus once more on the cries of those who are most often ignored, marginalized and dismissed as unworthy or unimportant. We seem to be erasing that critical virtue from our secular imagination. Our post-modern trend is to forget anything and everyone that stands in the way of our obsession with material progress and economic supremacy.

Our religious traditions call us back to *anamnesis*, the duty to remember. The Hebrew Scriptures remind us to remember the widow and the orphan, the stranger and alien, because "you, too, were once aliens in the land of Egypt" (Exodus 22:21; Deuteronomy 10:19; Leviticus 19:34). This is more than an ethical command; it is an appearance of the personality of Yahweh whose heart breaks, whose spirit is torn by the sound of those who are abused and oppressed. Our solidarity with the poor is an extension of our solidarity with the divine.

It is true in the ministry of Jesus. He turns our focus away from religious ritual and a rote observance of the Law, without dismissing their importance, so that we attend once again to all those falling through the cracks of society in the mad pursuit of religious righteousness and

[1] David B. Couturier, "Seminarians and Social Justice: A Psychological Investigation for Admission to Orders," *Laurentianum* 26 (1985), 31-72.

purity. Jesus lived in a time of hot tempers as the people waited anxiously and expectantly for a political Messiah to overthrow Rome and reinstall Yahweh's reign in Israel. They believed that purity, religious righteousness and strict observance of the Law were required before the Messiah could come. Anyone who could not or would not observe the law was not only unclean but they were also obstacles to Yahweh's agenda for the return of religious power in Israel. Anyone caught in this religious obstructionism had to be rejected.

Jesus' ministry was a calculated attempt to demonstrate the political and religious weakness of these false messianic claims. Jesus rejected the strategy that would use religious violence to overthrow the political violence of Rome. Jesus rightly calculated that "those who live by the sword will die by the sword." Instead Jesus threw his lot in with the lost and forsaken, the prostitutes and tax collectors.

He became the Victim of Rome's madness, brutality and violence. He took upon Himself the sins of the nation. His voice, his cry of abandonment on the Cross and his submission to the will of the Father, is the cry of all victims of every age. In that cry we can hear how evil works against innocence. We see how the wicked pursue the vulnerable and make them the scapegoated victims of injustice in order to appease the fears, desires and anxieties of others. In that cry we hear our own ongoing complicities with the strategies by which society dispels and dismisses those who are inconvenient in the pursuit of power, those we design as "permissible victims" and collateral damage in our hardened but often hidden agenda for domination and deprivation.

Jesus' cry reverberates down through the ages. His innocence is complete. Those who took him to trial could find no evidence against him and so they fabricated charges. The world's powers executed an innocent man on Calvary. When we peer into the wounds of that moment in time, we see the wounds of every age that precede and succeed it. We see humanity's domination and deprivation in those wounds. We hear in the cries of Calvary the cries of the men, women and children of every age who have been sucked into and swept up in the failed "alarms of armies that clash by night." We hear the insanity and the futility of our manic pursuit of power and privilege and the desperate attempts of the "widows and orphans" to avoid and escape it.

No other saint in history understood the moment of the Crucified as did Francis of Assisi. It was the voice of the Crucified, the voice of the Victim, that first spoke to him as a young and disturbed man in the ruined church of San Damiano. Francis had come home from war a lost and broken young man. His dreams had failed. His hopes for a life of nobility and glory had collapsed on the blood-soaked fields of

Collestrada. His redemption depended on hearing the cry of the Victim at San Damiano.

Francis intuits the meaning of that vision and goes in pursuit of the lepers outside of town and down in the valley from Assisi. He embraces them and begins a life of humble service to them. Though he spent his adolescence in absolute disgust and dismissal of the lepers, now he hears their voices. They are the victims of a horrible and disfiguring disease, but more than that, they are the victims of religious disdain, abandonment, and isolation. They are the victims of a cruel religious irony – the church's refusal to be in communion with them, the church's ritual to absolve itself of any further action or ministry with and among them.

As I have said in this book, Francis "reverses the negative" in his encounter with the leper. It seems that his gratitude toward the lepers comes from their willingness to embrace him. Francis had a provocative phrase for his condition at this time, "when I was in sin." It is Francis' signal of a deep moral and spiritual alienation from himself and from God. It is not a reference to a specific sin or particular moral transgression. It is his alienated and depraved condition. It connects to the arrogance and disgust he showed toward the lepers and anyone who was sick and vulnerable. Francis would pinch his nose from miles away and dismiss them from his consciousness, as he moved on in his pursuit of pride and glory.

Francis' redemption depended upon his ability to hear the cries of the lepers and make them his own. This would be the struggle of his life.

It was the spiritual test he would have to overcome at the end of his life. As Joseph Chinnici masterfully demonstrates, Francis is coming to the last stage of his life profoundly demoralized and depressed that he has failed his mission in life. The brothers have rejected him and his movement seems to be in ruins. He is angry and despondent. He is suffering from a botched surgery to fix his eyesight, a fitting metaphor for his failing vision for the fraternal economy that he started twenty years before.

He comes to La Verna a desperate and fragile man who is losing his faith, hope and love. Christ visits Him again, as He once did when Francis was a young man. Christ comes not in power and privilege and not in pride and glory. He comes as the crucified One, as the Victim who suffers in love for humankind. Francis must hear the Voice of the Victim once again. He must integrate what is being revealed to Him, in the same way and with the same intensity with which he heard it as a young man, long before the brothers grew in numbers and dispersed. The Victim reminds Francis to accept his wounds, to embrace his fragility, because God has embraced them. God has used Francis' weaknesses for God's own glory and hidden purposes. As noted before, the Crucified doesn't simply console Francis; He affirms him in the work he has performed, in the sufferings he has endured and in the love he has shared, even with and among the brothers who are rejecting him.

Francis receives the love of the seraph and becomes the crucified victim himself. The wounds of the victims manifested on his body are the outward signs of the reality that now mark Francis' soul. He has heard the voice of the victims, the cries of the lepers and the hurts of his brothers. Their wounds have become his wounds. Like Christ, Francis manifests in bodily form the wounds of the victims of his time, place and culture. He manifests them because he has allowed himself to be suffused with love, as is the seraph that visits him at the end of his life.

And here we find the project of our renewal.

If our church is to survive this great moment of tribulation, it must look deeply into the wounds of its own victims and all victims of injustice. It must turn its focus away from those who hawk power and privilege and hear the voices of victims, without trying to silence, muffle, distract or dismiss them. The scandal of the church is that it failed those it should have listened to first and foremost. By neglecting children who were abused, the Church abandoned Lazarus at the gate and walked past the Jew thrown into the ditch.

The Church must come back to its senses and its original purpose as "the community of the Beloved." The Church's long obsession with power and privilege, its defensive posture after the Reformation and its almost exclusive theological focus on the dynamics of Holy Orders have failed. The abused are its victims. The structures built up in defense of clerical position and privilege must be dismantled. We need new structures of collaboration, cooperation, accountability, transparency and equity between women and men, laity and clerics, the rich and the poor in the church.

We will begin this project when we hear the voice of the Victims, those who have been marginalized, excluded, dismissed and neglected, first of all. They are not our church's luxury items that we get to, when we find the time, when it becomes more convenient, after we do all the other "essential" things that need to be done as church in the post-modern world. The work of victims is the work of the church; their voice is the voice of God today. God speaks in no other language. God is understood in no other medium than in the cries of the dismissed, despised and deprived. The cry from the Cross is the cry of victims.

The voice of victims is the voice of God today. It is the voice of the Crucified. It must become the voice of the Church.

Index

A

B

C

D

E

F

G

H

I

J

L

Bibliography

Brueggemann, Walter. *Peace* [Understanding Biblical Themes Series] (St. Louis, MO: Chalice Press, 2001).

Chinnici, Joseph P., *When Values Collide: The Catholic Church, Sexual Abuse, and the Challenges of Leadership* (Maryknoll, NY: Orbis Books, 2010).

________________ "Passing on the Seal of Franciscan Life," *Franciscan Connections* 68:4 (Winter, 2018) 4-21.

Couturier, David B., *Franciscans and their Finances: Economics in a Disenchanted World* (St. Bonaventure, NY: Franciscan Institute Publications, 2015).

Dalarun, Jacques. *The Canticle of Brother Sun: Francis of Assisi Reconciled.* Philippe Yates, trans. (St. Bonaventure, NY: Franciscan Institute Publications, 2014).

Dietsch, Nancy. *Soul Reintegration for Post Traumatic Growth: A Meaning-Centered Approach to Healing through Logotherapy Lived* (Doctoral Dissertation: Graduate Theological Foundation, 2014).

Esposito, Elizabeth A. *Embodying Mysticism: The Utilization of Embodied Experience in the Mysticism of Italian Women, Circa 1200-1400 CE* (MA Thesis, University of Florida, 2004).

Lamb, Matthew L., *Solidarity with Victims: Toward a Theology of Social Transformation* (New York: Crossroads, 1982).

Massingale, Bryan. N., *Racial Justice and the Catholic Church* (Maryknoll NY: Orbis Books, 2010);

________________ "Vox Victimarum. Vox Dei: Malcolm X as Neglected "Classic" for Catholic Theological Reflection," *Proceedings of the Catholic Theological Society of America* 65 (2010), 63-88.

Pryds, Darleen. *Enduring Presence: Diversity and Authenticity among the First Generations of Franciscan Laity* (St. Bonaventure, NY: Franciscan Institute Publications, 2018).

Van Deusen Hunsinger, Deborah. *Bearing the Unbearable: Trauma, Gospel and Pastoral Care* (Grand Rapids, MI: Eerdmans, 2015).